Garden **TOOLS**

Garden TOOLS

VAL BRADLEY & JOHN NEGUS

CARROLL & BROWN PUBLISHERS LIMITED

I wish to dedicate this book to my dear wife, Phyll, who supported and encouraged me throughout our life together.
John Negus

First published in 2001 in the United Kingdom by:

Carroll & Brown Publishers Limited
20 Lonsdale Road
Queen's Park
London NW6 6RD

Editor Helen Griffin

Art Editor Vimit Punater

Photography David Murray and Jules Selmes

Illustrations and compilation © 2001 Carroll & Brown Limited

Text © 2001 Val Bradley and John Negus

A CIP catalogue record for this book is available from the British Library.

ISBN 1-903258-23-5

Reproduced by P. T. Repro Multi Warna, Jakarta
Printed and bound by Book Print, Barcelona
First edition

Contents

Introduction 6

1 Digging In 8

2 Cultivating the Soil 24

3 Controlling the Environment 38

4 Cutting and Trimming 54

5 Planting and Sowing 80

6 Tidying the Garden 94

7 Working Safely 116

8 Gardening with Ease 130

9 Looking after Your Tools 144

Glossary 152
Acknowledgements 153
Picture Credits and Suppliers 154
Index 156

Introduction

Ask anyone who has been gardening for a while about their favourite tool and they will always have one. It might be a brand new implement which makes working easier, but it's just as likely to be one passed down from another keen gardener in the family. Many a gardener has a treasured family spade, for instance, which has been repaired so much over the years – with a new handle here and a new head there – that it is actually a completely different implement. Yet to its owner it will still feel like the same old, much-loved spade.

To the uninitiated, the selection of tools available today can be vast and bewildering. Even an apparently simple item, such as a hand trowel, comes in an enormous array. What is the optimum shape and size? Is there any advantage in choosing one kind of blade over another? What kind of handle should it have?

Selecting the best tool for each job means that you can execute the task with minimum effort and maximum pleasure. This book explains the tasks each tool performs well, so you don't struggle with the wrong one, and details how to use it. The first few chapters look at implements for all the important tasks in the garden: digging (Chapter 1); cultivating and weeding (Chapter 2); watering, reading the weather and greenhouse equipment (Chapter 3); cutting and trimming the lawn and your plants (Chapter 4); planting and sowing (Chapter 5); and tidying the garden (clearing, hauling and composting: Chapter 6). Safety is the subject of Chapter 7, which covers such issues as wearing protective gear, working with electricity and chemicals and ensuring the garden is safe when children or pets are around. And Chapters 8 and 9 offer advice on tools that make your life easier, and maintenance and storage respectively. Interspersed throughout are features on specialist tools for hobbyists (such as bonsai, water gardens and roses).

Whether you are building a collection from scratch or simply looking to add to or get the most from your existing tool kit, we hope that this book will help you to ensure that gardening is always a source of pleasure and never a chore.

1

Digging In

Improving the soil

Ever since our ancestors began to grow plants for food, they recognized the need to cultivate the soil. The simple fact is that plants grow better in properly prepared ground. The earliest cultivation tools included sticks and large animal bones. But successive generations have refined the tools to the spades, shovels, forks and mattocks that we use today.

The best way of improving most soils is to take a spade to them and start digging. The purpose of turning the sod, whether it is to one spade's depth (a process known as 'single digging') or two ('double digging') is to put air into it, and whether you enjoy the task or dread it, turning soil is a necessary part of the gardening year.

WHY DO YOU NEED TO DIG?

Air is critical to plant roots, and without it the plants would die. A lack of air in the soil is often caused by compaction, which occurs naturally, particularly in areas of high rainfall or where land is often trodden.

Digging and turning the soil, especially in the autumn, enables the freezing action of winter frosts to break down larger clumps and create new air pockets between the particles making the soil easier for the roots to penetrate. It plays an important part in the organic cycle within the soil, allowing the burying of crop and plant debris, weeds and organic wastes, such as manure or garden compost.

It also aids beneficial soil organisms, such as worms and bacteria, which must have air in order to live. These creatures break down organic waste and open up the soil further to incorporate more air and allow rainwater to drain away more freely.

Drainage is an important consideration if you live in an area where the level of rainfall is high, or on a heavy, clay soil that is prone to waterlogging. Regular digging is essential to the structure of these soils and should be done on an annual basis wherever possible – especially in highly productive areas such as the vegetable patch. In an established shrub border, where the plants are to remain in place for a number of years, it is more important to prepare the ground thoroughly before planting begins.

Weeping roses are given form and structure by using an 'umbrella' or 'basket' frame. Secure your rose to a central column and, using soft string, tie the shoots to the frame. Lightly prune a weeping standard with a sharp pair of pruning shears.

Building up and cutting down

Wrap your roses in horticultural crop-protection fleece for the winter (above), and be sure to cover any young shoots if there are frosts forecast. Use shears (above left) or loppers to tackle those with thick stems.

rotating handle. These reduce the strain on your wrist as well as the risk of blisters, and they make pruning that much more enjoyable.

Periodically, tough old shoots need clipping to spur new growth from the base. Use strong loppers rather than secateurs. Choose a pair with lightweight aluminium handles and a cantilever cutting action to increase leverage.

The best saw to prune the limbs off rose shrubs is a safe, fold-up version with a high-carbon and non-clogging steel blade and a set of precision-ground, razor-sharp teeth. Buy one with a safety catch to secure the blade.

Rose training

Reminiscent of a skeletal, wire hanging basket, with or without a central pole, a rose trainer is positioned over the head of a standard weeping rose to provide ornamental support. New shoots tied to it are trained to form an umbrella of flowering branches.

Classical obelisks are pillars entwined with the spiralling shoots of climbing roses in various heights and diameters. The best modern types use plastic-coated 3-cm steel

tubing linked with metal rings and are topped with a moulded finial.

Twine is essential for tying in young stems – they should be trained as horizontally as possible to encourage a wealth of blossom. It's best to use organic, jute twine, which can then be composted when you replace it.

Whenever you work with roses, you must wear heavy-duty, thornproof gloves to guard against lacerating your fingers. You should also wear safety goggles as shoots can fly from your grasp and into your face. Choose a pair with adjustable arms and lenses.

Knapsack sprayer

Most roses need spraying with fungicide and insecticide. The most efficient way to do this is with a pump-up, knapsack sprayer. Contoured to fit your back, it comes with a heavy-duty pump handle to reduce effort. Accessories include an extension lance and fan spray nozzle.

Propagation

If you're keen to increase a hybrid tea rose variety that is budded on to a stock plant, you'll need a sharp, flat-bladed budding knife with a thumb grip. It should have a flat-ended handle for prising up the T-shaped cut you make in the bark to insert the bud.

need to germinate, but even if some do start to grow, they seldom have the energy to push through the extra depth of soil and reach the surface. An important tip is to work backwards rather than forwards: turning the soil introduces air into it, but by standing on it too quickly you can squash the air straight back out, leaving it compacted.

DOUBLE DIGGING

Also known as deep digging, this process of aerating and amending the soil is especially useful on heavy clay soils that form sticky lumps and resist all efforts to break them into a fine tilth with crumbly texture. It is best carried out in the autumn so that winter frosts can break down larger clods for you.

As the name suggests, this technique involves digging down to the depth of two spade blades instead of just one. To double dig, you need to excavate a spade-deep trench, putting the soil to one side, and then dig down for another spade's depth to work the soil at the bottom of the trench. Next, you dig a second trench, adjacent to the first one, turning the topsoil you excavate from this into the previous trench. Once you have loosened the subsoil at the bottom of this second trench, you can use the soil from the first one to fill the last one (for step-by-step instructions, see below).

The soil at the bottom of the trench is known as subsoil; this is a much less fertile medium but it holds most moisture. For good plant growth, roots must penetrate this subsoil to keep them supplied with water, even in summer.

Keep topsoil and subsoil separate at all times as you are working. Mixing them together will not improve the fertility of the subsoil – as was believed for a time – but it will dilute that of the topsoil.

OTHER USES

The spade is a versatile tool, and you don't just have to use it for digging; it is also helpful for moving quantities of soil or compost around the garden, or for skimming the turf or weeds off the surface of an area before you construct the base of a new building or dig out a pond. Do this by holding the spade so that it is almost parallel to the ground and sliding it under the top inch of the soil with quick, sharp pushes. You can reuse any turf you take off in this manner elsewhere in the garden.

The weight of the spade makes it a handy tool for activities like breaking up clods and tapping down soil and paving stones – be careful not to damage it, though. The straight cutting blade can be used to create neat-edged borders, to cut through weeds and to prise up rocks and stones.

Double digging

1 **MARKING OUT** Start by marking out the area to be dug, as you will be working up one side and back down the other.

2 **DIG A TRENCH** Follow the instructions for single digging (page 13), but instead of replacing the topsoil, put it into a wheelbarrow and keep it to one side.

3 **IMPROVE ROOT PENETRATION** Use a fork to loosen the subsoil at the bottom of the trench, pushing it down to the full depth of its tines. Lift the soil, then let it fall back, breaking it up by turning the fork over and using the prongs on any larger clods. This cultivates the soil to two blades' depth. Place a generous layer of well-rotted manure or garden compost onto the bottom of the trench.

4 **WORK ON THE SECOND TRENCH** Using the spade, dig the next trench, but this time throw the topsoil into the first trench, and mix it thoroughly with the compost or manure. Work around the plot until you reach the last trench, finishing off by using the topsoil taken from the first trench.

SHOVELS

This is a different implement depending upon which side of the Atlantic Ocean you garden. In the UK, a standard shovel is a wide, almost square-bladed implement used for moving larger quantities of material around than a spade will hold. You would seldom use it for 'proper' gardening activities and are more likely to find it useful when mixing concrete or moving organic matter. The Cornish spade is a long-handled shovel with a blade tapering to a point.

The American shovel closely resembles a traditional Cornish spade (from which it probably evolved with the early settlers), with a long, straight handle and a dished, pointed blade that can enter the soil with impressive force.

The shovel is most useful as a scooping tool, for which it is conveniently dish-shaped. Its concave blade holds soil more efficiently than the flatter spade, which is why it is the tool of choice for many gardeners. The pointed blade will cut through compacted soil more easily than the spade, but is probably less useful for pure digging because it does not produce a straight edge. It is a multi-functional tool, however, and can do anything a rectangular spade can do in terms of lifting, moving, planting, transplanting and mixing materials.

The shovel's long handle means that gardeners of any height can use it – unlike the spade handle, which is of a set length. It also allows you to shift your grip according to the weight you are lifting or the soil you are trying to cultivate.

To use a shovel, rest your foot on the tread of the blade, hold the shaft up vertically, and use your body weight to push the blade down into the soil. Then

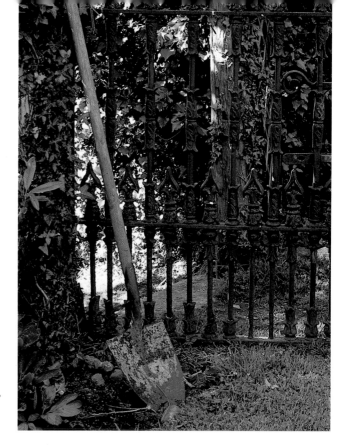

Happy shovelling

The long handle of the shovel allows you to adjust your grip as appropriate, while the wide, bowl-shaped dish enables you to carry material without spilling it.

stand up straight, and use the long handle as a lever, pulling it towards you to loosen the soil. Bend at the knees to pick up a small scoop, and then swivel at the hips to dispose of the material. Remember always to bend your legs rather than your back to avoid injury.

Use your shovel to move piles of soil, compost, plant matter such as grass clippings, sand or any other material. For comfort and efficiency, keep shovelfuls small and light, working regularly and, if possible, rapidly, to reduce the pile.

The best shovels have heads made from a single piece of forged steel that have been thickened at the points of greatest stress where the shovel might bend. If you have a choice of tread, opt for a forward-rolled tread, which will protect the soles of your boots from shock or stress during repeated digging.

WHAT CAN YOU DO WITH A SHOVEL?

- Loosen soil surface before planting or adding dry fertilizer
- Cultivate the soil
- Lift and throw substantial piles of organic matter
- Transplant and plant perennials and shrubs in the garden
- Mix concrete
- Slice finger-sized underground roots during digging

FORKS

The basic design of the fork is fairly universal, with a long, straight handle and four metal prongs or tines. The prongs vary according to the intended use of the fork: a digging fork has square-profile tines for the soil to cling to; the circular prongs of the pitch or hay fork help the soil slide off; and the flat tines in others such as the potato or beet fork avoid damage to the crop.

WHAT CAN YOU DO WITH A FORK?

- Loosen soil surface before planting or adding dry fertilizer
- Cultivate in confined spaces between fragile plants in the border
- Spike a lawn to improve drainage (before brushing in sand)
- Penetrate the bottom of a trench during double digging
- Lift and transport cartfuls of manure and other organic matter
- Lift root vegetables, including potatoes and carrots

Prongs are angled according to the fork's purpose – straight tines are best for digging and arched ones are more suited to scooping.

The so-called garden fork, with four prongs, is the heaviest-duty model, and the tool of choice for gardeners who do a lot of double digging. Spading, digging and border forks are similar to garden forks but smaller, lighter and a little less resilient. These make good all-purpose tools. Where space is restricted, a border fork is smaller and will fit between the plants more easily.

Other forks for lifting manure and bedding have between five and ten tines, and are used primarily for animal bedding and waste. However, they are quite useful in the garden for moving bulk quantities of material around, such as mulch, compost or leaves, or for lifting small root crops like new potatoes, which would fall through the gaps between the tines of a standard digging fork. Pitch forks tend to have just two or three long prongs and a long handle, perfect for lifting hay and lightweight mulches.

Use a potato fork to prise out root vegetables, like beets, carrots and potatoes from the soil. The five or six prongs are blunt, so won't damage the crop.

Like the spade, the fork serves several purposes. You would use a garden fork for loosening the soil's surface – where deep digging is not possible between established plants in the border – and especially when adding dry fertilizer to the upper layer of soil around plants. Always work backwards so that you do not stand on soil that has been dug over.

SPIKING A LAWN

You can instantly improve a poorly draining lawn area by 'spiking' it with a fork – simply drive the prongs down into the grass to their full depth with your foot. You can leave the resulting holes open or, for a more permanent solution, fill them with sand. Brush the sand over the lawn's surface making sure it goes down into the holes.

The fork is also ideal for rough levelling a cultivated area after you have dug it and before you start to lay turf, plant out or sow seed. However, final levelling is best done with a rake.

RELIEVING COMPACTION

Where the fork really comes into its own is for deep cultivation of the soil in 'double digging' (see page 16). The garden fork has a great ability to penetrate compacted layers of soil because each slender tine can exert tremendous pressure through its pointed tip. This allows you to break through the initial compaction, lift the soil and then break it into smaller clods. By turning the fork over and hitting the lumps of soil with the points of the tines, you can reduce the lumps to a manageable size.

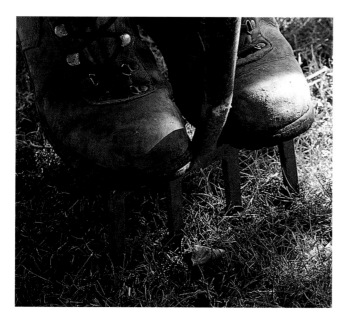

Aerating your lawn

Use your body weight on a garden fork to make holes in your lawn, then move the handle around slightly to enlarge them. Brush sand into the holes for good drainage.

MATTOCKS AND PICKS

Spades and forks are good for most digging purposes, but some jobs require an altogether tougher tool. This is where the mattock or pick comes in.

While not being the most-used tools in the garden shed, mattocks and picks will be invaluable at certain times in a larger garden. These are heavy-duty implements designed for cutting through solid soil or thick roots with ease, although in some parts of the world where the soil is thin and stony, a broad-bladed, hoe-like mattock is used in place of a spade for basic cultivation.

The difference between these two implements lies in their shape. The pick has a stout wooden handle and a metal head with two pointed ends, one sharp, the other squared. It is an ideal implement for digging a trench, especially through compacted, stony ground. Raise it and swing it down in a circular motion, with one hand remaining at the base of the handle while the other slides up and down to control the swing.

In contrast, the head of the mattock has one chisel-pointed end, whilst the other is flattened into a cutting blade. It is a combination of useful cultivator for stony areas and sturdy tool for lifting or cutting through stubborn roots or brambles.

The standard mattock can perform a variety of cultivating tasks. It can dig in and break up soil, cut through obstructive roots, and push or pull rocks and stones out of the way. More specialized mattocks are also available from some manufacturers. Short-handled bedding mattocks have a pointed, trowel-shaped head to make a plant-size hole in the soil; and certain models have a fork-like head with narrow tines, which are useful for breaking up clumps of soil without gathering up soil.

Both tools require a reasonable amount of strength to use, and good technique is essential if you are to avoid injury. Work with a steady rhythm to avoid jerking and straining your back, and be sure to keep a tight hold of the handle.

Checking the connection

Picks gather a good deal of force as you swing them in a circular motion, so make sure the connection between head and shaft is firm – or you may be in for a shock!

CHOOSING THE RIGHT TOOLS

To do any physical job properly – with a minimum of impact to your body – it is essential to have a tool that suits both you and the work you are planning to undertake. A tall person cannot work efficiently when employing a short-handled spade and, equally, a small-framed person will find the job much harder if using a large, heavy spade.

Before buying a digging tool, such as a spade or fork, there are a number of things to find out and consider. The first thing to be done, if at all possible, is to practise with the tools themselves to gauge their weight and balance.

Look for a combination of strength and lightness. Try borrowing tools from gardening friends who have experience in using them, or visit a range of tool centres and try as many different makes as possible for weight and balance. Hold them, bend over with them, lift them – in fact, all the things you would do if you buy them. Don't worry about looking foolish in the store – the right tool is an investment and needs appropriate research, while the wrong tool could cause you hours of painful backache.

In each case, the straight handle connects to the heavy head by passing through an 'eye' in the centre of the head itself. This means that if the handle is damaged, you can easily replace it. You should check the shaft regularly, particularly if it is made of wood, to ensure it is smooth and free of splinters. Dry it carefully before putting it into storage to prevent the wood from rotting or shrinking. If the handle shows any sign at all of shrinking within the eye, replace it, because the last thing you'll need is the head flying off while the tool is in use.

Strong joints

Digging implements are subject to considerable pressure, so it is important that the blade or head is firmly attached to the handle. The two strongest joints are the socket (right) and the saddle (far right).

A comfortable handle will enable you to work more efficiently. The T-handle (bottom of picture) is best for pushing against, whereas the D-handle (middle) is easier to twist. YD-handles (top) are generally made of wood, so if you prefer to garden without gloves, this type of grip is a good choice.

CHOOSE HANDLES WITH CARE

Examine the shaft of the implement to check that all of the surfaces are smooth, as this will help to avoid injury to your hands. Pay particular attention to the handle or grip, as a smooth, well-made handle will greatly reduce the risk of painful blisters as you work. Handles with a Y- or T-shaped grip have been around since the days of the Roman Empire. Most heavy-duty garden tools today have D-, YD- (wishbone-shaped), or T-shaped handles, and the one you choose will be a matter of comfort and personal preference (see also caption, above). Try the grip for size before you buy the implement, because a narrow one may be difficult to use if you prefer to work with gardening gloves, and a chunky one may be too large if you have small hands. Ergonomic grips to make working easier are angled forwards slightly, away from the body.

The grip itself may be made of weather-proofed wood (usually ash), tubular metal or polypropylene (which may have an integral moulded grip). Modern polypropylene grips are molded in one continuous hollow piece by gas injection. They are smooth, strong and created at an ideal digging angle. They can even be stabilized against UV and recycled.

WHAT SIZE OF TOOL?

Spades and forks come in three basic sizes: small, medium and large. The smallest is known as a border size; the medium as ladies' size or medium; and the largest is digging size. The size you choose will depend on you and your garden. If your garden is large and needs a lot of maintenance, then your tools will have to be big and strong enough to cope. If, on the other hand, your garden is small and confined, then the tools will have to be correspondingly smaller and a border size may be more suitable.

Choose a size and weight that you can work with comfortably for as long as it takes to finish the job. Some manufacturers have taken into account the

JOINTS

Look at the joint between the head (the tines of a fork or the blade of a spade) and the handle. Check that it is firm and secure, or the two may part company as you are working.

There are two main methods of attaching the head to the shaft: the socket joint and the saddle joint. Both types of attachment are strong and should withstand years of heavy use.

With a socket joint, the handle fits into a circular hole at the top of the head, and is secured in place with rivets driven through the shaft. A socket fitting may be long or short; the longer the socket, the less handle there will be, and the stronger the implement. Lipped sockets have a short strap at the front and back to increase their strength.

In the case of the saddle joint, two straps come up from the head and lie against the front and back of the handle, secured with two or more rivets.

You may come across tools where the head is a cut-out piece of metal that has been folded into shape around the handle, leaving a hollow indentation at the back. This design is unlikely to be expensive – but will probably not last very long. It may be ideal for building sand castles on the beach, but it's best to avoid it for the garden.

THE MAKING OF SPADES

Metal garden tools, which date back to Roman times, would once have been the province of the local craftsman-cum-blacksmith. He would have been able to melt down and reuse broken tools to make new ones.

Mass production of garden tools began in the 19th century in response to the huge interest in gardening as a leisure pursuit. The big advances in manufacture since have been in the materials used to produce the tools, which have dramatically reduced their weight. The design has changed just slightly, although it is now possible to buy tools with a built-in grip for the foot to press down on, to make digging easier.

Many tools today are made of carbon steel, a mixture of carbon and mild steel which is heat-treated and tempered for strength. Mild steel alone would rust overnight without protection.

Hand-forging spades

Made using techniques passed down by generations of blacksmiths, handmade spades and hoes are in great demand for their quality and durability.

1 **THE BASIC SHAPE** First, stainless steel spade heads are clipped into shape, ready to be put in the fire.

2 **HEATING THE METAL** The heads are then fired until red-hot and suitably malleable to be beaten and moulded.

3 **THE HARDENING PROCESS** To withstand heavy use, the blade has to be hardened by means of compression, followed by heat and rapid cooling. The tool is then dipped in acid leaving it shiny and new.

gradual increase in average height of the population, and offer a range of tools suited to taller gardeners. Their longer length encourages a more upright working stance and reduces the risk of backache. Spades and shovels are available with a straight shaft up to almost 2 metres long and, as well as suiting taller people, these are useful for providing good leverage during deeper digging.

THE TOOL HEAD

Digging tools are generally made from steel, which comes in various types and grades (see right). Top-of-the-range tools are generally made from stainless steel, but high-carbon models are also good quality and won't set you back as much.

Tempered or forged implements are preferable over stamped ones (which are machine cut and bent to the required shape) as they are better designed to withstand hard use.

When buying tools, look to see if the head is coated. Many carbon-steel heads are given a special epoxy paint coating to lengthen their lifetime. As well as reducing the chance of soil sticking to the head, this coating will make the tool lighter and easier to use. It should also guard against rust, scratching and the effects of humidity and alkalis in the soil.

COUNTING THE COST

The final consideration is one of cost, and in this instance, you really do get what you pay for. If you have a tiny garden, which is largely made up of hard surfaces and with just a small area of planting to be looked after, then it is unlikely to be worth your while spending a fortune on stainless-steel tools. If your garden is large or you intend to produce and maintain a viable vegetable patch, then cheaper tools are likely to last for perhaps three seasons before they bend or

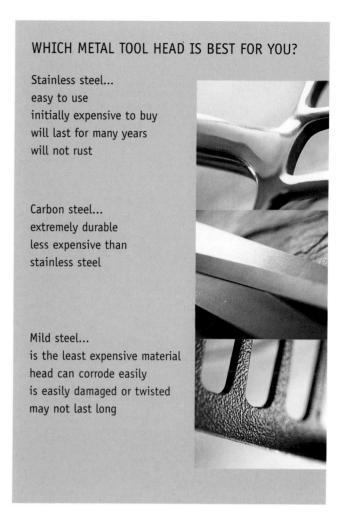

WHICH METAL TOOL HEAD IS BEST FOR YOU?

Stainless steel...
easy to use
initially expensive to buy
will last for many years
will not rust

Carbon steel...
extremely durable
less expensive than
stainless steel

Mild steel...
is the least expensive material
head can corrode easily
is easily damaged or twisted
may not last long

break. It all depends on how much you use the tools and for what. Used correctly, stainless steel tools (the most expensive option) should last you a lifetime and will be a good investment. They also make a wonderful present for the new gardener who is just starting out. For advice on how to look after your tools, whatever their shape or material, turn to Chapter 9 (pages 146–51).

>tools of the **future**

The days of wooden tools may be numbered. Manufacturers are looking at the possibility of using plastics to form the whole implement, not just the handle. From their point of view, the problem is that these tools would have a much longer life and would be almost indestructible. Great news for the consumer though!

2

Cultivating the Soil

Tools for weeding

One square metre of soil can hold an average of 50 000 viable seeds a year, and as soon as you break the surface of the soil, seeds in the upper layers receive the daylight they need to germinate. Add to these the weeds that creep under the fence from your neighbour's garden, and those the birds leave behind as they fly over, and you will have a good crop of weeds in your garden!

CULTIVATING GOOD HABITS

Once you start to cultivate your soil, you must continue, but a little-and-often approach means that it need not become a battle. It is up to you to ensure that weed seedlings do not compete for the limited light, moisture and nutrients available for the plants that you do want to grow. The best way to make sure of this is to cultivate the soil around your plants using hoes, rakes, cultivators, trowels and hand forks.

Well-made joints

Hoes, rakes and cultivators with wooden (usually ash) handles all tend to have a tang-and-ferrule fitting for extra strength, with the joint just above the head. Where the shaft is aluminium or polypropylene, the joint is a socket fitting. Whichever you choose, make

---

UNDERSTANDING THE ORGANIC CYCLE

The plants that start to grow send their questing roots down into the first covering, sucking up moisture and breaking down the bedrock further. When they die, they decay into organic matter that feeds both the new plants and the organisms in the soil. When the organisms die, they, in turn, form nutrients that the plants can use. The leaves that fall from the plants form a natural mulch over the soil and are gradually taken down and incorporated into the soil by the organisms that dwell there. This cycle is repeated every year, building up the soil unless there is some outside interference to affect the process.

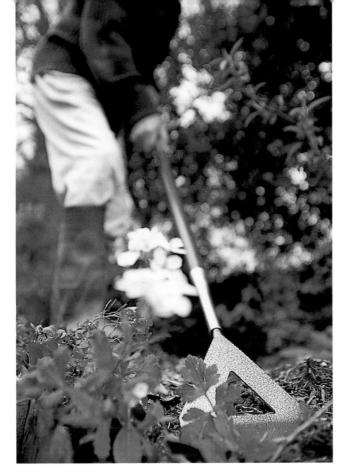

Handling a hoe

The perennially popular Dutch hoe is used with a push-pull action. It cuts weeds down to size before they start to compete for nutrients and moisture with plants you want to grow. Ensure your hoe is light enough to be wielded by your arms rather than by your back, which should be kept straight.

and the ferrule is a metal ring that is designed to be fitted down over the joint to hold it closed and prevent the wood from parting.

HOES

The humble hoe is a versatile implement, ideal for light, regular, ground cultivation. Use it to control weeds and loosen the soil around the base of plants. Most have a long, straight handle with a metal head, but there are many designs from around the world that were developed to take account of local conditions. The three most common designs are: the Dutch hoe, the draw (or swan-neck) hoe and the triangular-headed hoe.

Which you use will be a matter of personal preference as much as a selection based on technical use. There may even be regional variation, with local history and soil conditions dictating what is available for purchase. The Dutch hoe is a good starting point for general gardening, as it can cope with most soils, from a light sandy loam to a fairly heavy clay, and can be turned slightly so that the corner of the blade will make an adequate drill if you want to sow seed. If you are growing vegetables or have lumpy soil, you may wish to add a draw hoe to your collection, as it is useful for breaking clods, earthing up, and will produce a finer drill for sowing small seeds.

WHEELED HOE

This device is for the gardener who wishes to cultivate a large area, because it is not easy to manoeuvre between closely spaced plants. It has a lightweight

sure that the joint is tight and well-made. A poor fitting will not last long and may part company just when you least wish it. When considering a hoe, rake or cultivator, ensure that the tool is light enough for your arms to wield it (rather than your back) and that the handle is a comfortable length. Tools are generally lightweight, and the heads are made of stainless steel or carbon steel and coated with a protective epoxy paint. This coating makes the tool easier to handle by reducing soil adhesion.

What to look for in a hand tool

The shaft may be treated wood (usually ash), aluminium, or polypropylene – and the grip, if there is one, is usually polypropylene. The head may be attached to the shaft with a socket fitting (where the head has a circular hole into which the shaft is pushed and held in place with rivets) or, where the shaft is wood, a tang-and-ferrule. The tang is a sharp point on the top of the head that fits into the base of the shaft

'Whatever hour the sun may say, it's always time for weeding;
The dandelion which blooms today, tomorrow will be seeding.'
A.A. MILNE, WRITER AND POET (1882–1956)

Bonsai tools

Bonsai, or the ancient Eastern art of dwarfing trees, is not a hobby to hurry. It can take a lifetime of commitment to truly understand this complex and beautiful art form. But knowing the right tools to use can give you a head start.

The addictive art form of bonsai was pioneered in the Far East, around 1000 years ago, and literally means 'a tree' (*sai*) 'growing in glazed terracotta tray or pot' (*bon*). The challenge is to replicate in miniature the trunk, shoots, leaves and flowers of a tree, bush or climber that, in struggling to survive in the cleft of a rock, has become gnarled, contorted and curiously beautiful.

Good contenders are trees such as maple, Japanese white pine, Chinese elm, Chinese juniper, crab apple, azalea, beech and hornbeam. They will, given dedication, grow to awesome veterans: a centenarian bonsai pine is not uncommon, believe it or not.

The key to keeping a tree small, healthy and mimicking its ancient, craggy wildwood cousin, is the care you give it. Prune it regularly and train its shoots, shorten its roots and periodically repot it. Initially, you will need only branch cutters to shape it but, as your sculpture matures, you'll need other specialist tools to prune, form and tweak it.

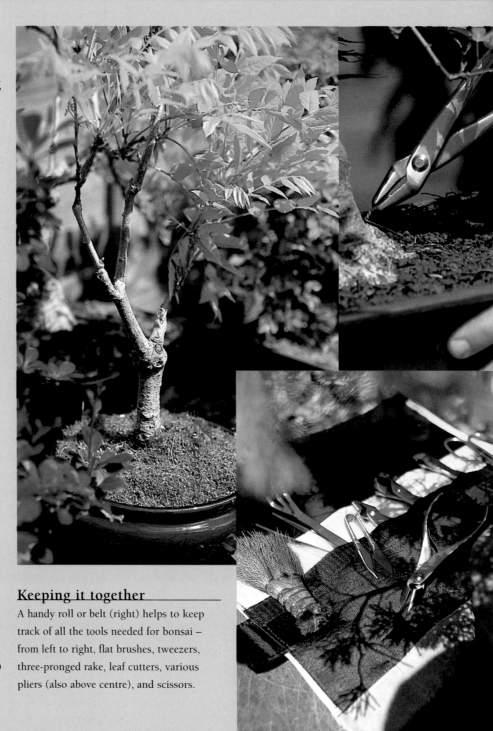

Clipping and cutting
To shape the tree, invest in a pair of branch cutters. Concave branch cutters are best for removing branches very close to the trunk, to avoid leaving a stump. They also

Keeping it together
A handy roll or belt (right) helps to keep track of all the tools needed for bonsai – from left to right, flat brushes, tweezers, three-pronged rake, leaf cutters, various pliers (also above centre), and scissors.

A delicate business

Tweezers (far left) are ideal for the intricate work of weeding the pot and removing any pests. Once the tree is established, a sharp chisel (left) can be employed to carve realistic gouges or to whittle out channels and veins.

Tools called jin pliers are designed to strip bark to simulate the dead, bleached shoots caused by weather and lightning. You will also need a pair of pliers to manipulate the training wire, and long-handled wire cutters, with sharp, chunky jaws, which will bite through wire without harming bark or tissue.

Make sure you've got a good pair of scissors in your tool kit. Use a large-handled, thin-bladed pair to remove shoots, branches and thin roots and a long, thin-handled pair with narrow blades to cut off slender shoots and twigs sprouting from the crown of a tree.

Reminiscent of large tweezers with sheep-shear blades, leaf cutters can also be used for removing soft leafy shoots.

Tools for fine work

For nipping out young shoots or removing pests, such as caterpillars and greenfly, it is always very useful to have a good pair of tweezers handy.

For cleaning the soil, a flattened shaving brush with flexible bristles is ideal for sprucing up the surface and cleaning mud-splashed trays.

Separating matted roots when moving or resetting plants can be a tricky procedure. Short and stocky, with a tapered and grippable handle, the three-pronged rake is ideal for this task.

Shaping up

Actively manipulating the shape of a living tree requires some flexible tools. There's no better way of contorting a straight branch to make it look old and interesting than by binding it with one of several thicknesses of anodized aluminium wire.

You could also try the screw clamp. Comprised of two screw hooks, butterfly nuts, a metal bar and a screw bolt with a clamp, it's invaluable for bending a branch or trunk without breaking it. With this gadget's help, you can simulate many fanciful shapes – arching or contorted, as from a river cliff.

To separate two closely spaced branches and improve a tree's shape, the best way is to push them apart with a length of wood with a V-shaped cut at each end.

In nature, lightning can tear a limb from the trunk. In bonsai, you can simulate natural wounds by gouging out lumps of bark with a very sharp wood chisel.

Potting your tree

The container should complement the tree it is holding. Trees with rounded crowns look best in oval pots. Pines, junipers and azaleas all need very deep pots, and pines and junipers also need unglazed pots; most other plants do well in glazed pots.

Clamping its style

The tree clamp (above) manipulates the shape of stiff trunks and branches that do not respond to wiring. It has two hooks that can be adjusted to exert pressure on the tree.

help the cut heal more quickly and neatly than secateurs. Knob cutters can also be used for taking off branches close to the trunk and removing trunk knobs and roots.

To trim off larger branches, a pull saw is the best tool to use. Cutting on the pull stroke reduces binding and improves the smoothness of the overall cut.

frame, with two handles, like a bicycle, leading down to a single wheel with a pneumatic tyre (filled with compressed air) to absorb impact.

Behind the wheel-hoe blade is a fitting for various interchangeable attachments like an oscillating head or a tined cultivator that will loosen the upper 10 cm of soil, disturbing any germinating weed seedlings. This is useful wherever plants grow in rows spaced widely enough for the user to pass without touching or damaging them, such as a larger vegetable patch. Any aeration value tends to be lost as the user walks behind the tool.

DRAW HOE

You can use the draw hoe with a pulling or chopping action to break up the soil. It is very effective at removing weeds and their roots, especially tap roots, or for thinning seedlings. It has a flat blade attached to the shaft with a curved neck. To use it, stand beside the area being hoed and move either backwards or forwards. Turned upside down, the curved swan neck is useful for making a seed drill.

TRIANGULAR-HEADED HOE

You should use the triangular-headed hoe in a pulling action for making a shallow drill along a straight line, rather than routine cultivations and weed removal.

Once the seeds have been sown in the drill, pull the soil gently back over them using the back of the blade. This less-common hoe allows spot-weeding between closely planted seedlings and in the border, without kneeling or bending.

THE DUTCH HOE

The Dutch or scuffle hoe is easy to use and has a sharp, angled blade at the leading edge of a D-shaped head. You can use it to cultivate the upper layer of soil by making short, sharp, push-pull strokes at a 20–30 degree angle and walking backwards. This uproots small weed seedlings leaving them to wither on the surface or to be removed by hand for disposal.

Hoe, hoe, hoe

Modern hoes have evolved to suit specific soil conditions and needs. The most popular styles are the draw hoe (top); the triangular-headed hoe (centre above); Dutch hoe (centre right); and oscillating hoe (bottom).

Rake's progress

Use the rake in a forwards and backwards motion, keeping your back straight. Remove weeds, pebbles and unearthed debris to create a finely crumbled seed bed.

OSCILLATING HOE

This is a double-action tool for removing weeds and loosening heavily compacted soil. It has a square-shaped head attached firmly to the shaft with a connection allowing it to rock back and forth in use. As both edges are sharp, this means that it can cut on the forward push and the backward pull, cutting weeds off below the soil's surface.

When should you hoe?

Hoeing is best when timed well. If the soil is too wet, you will create lumps and the weeds will resist your attempts to remove them. Too dry, and the surface will be hard to break through – and doing so will release moisture to evaporate. Aim to leave a finely broken soil texture that is clear of all weeds. Compost all weeds except those that are seeding or have root systems that could survive the process.

Once you have finished, clean any soil off the hoe and let it dry. Sharpen the blade with a file at least once a season to make sure it cuts easily as you work and give it a good wipe over with an oily cloth.

RAKES

The rake is a gathering implement, used since Roman times for the harvest. It can come in a variety of shapes and sizes and may have a metal or wooden

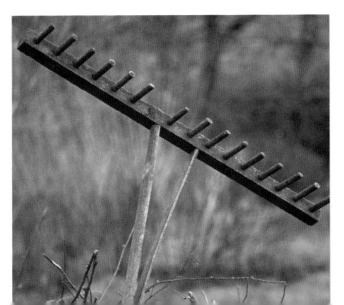

head. Early examples were made in a very practical fashion, with the teeth screwed into the head so that a broken one could be easily replaced. Even today, it is possible to find rakes with replaceable teeth, but they are more often cast as a single unit.

HOW TO USE THE RAKE

In the garden, you can use the rake for gathering stones, weeds and hedge clippings. It is a vital tool for levelling and preparing a seedbed – but you should handle it lightly. Do not allow the teeth to dig in too deeply or you will spoil the effect by dragging large clods back to the surface. A combination of repeated raking and treading are the only means of producing the kind of seedbed essential for a new lawn.

Use it with a backward-forward, push-pull motion, bracing yourself as you bend forwards and straighten. Try to work when the soil is moist so that any lumps of soil will break apart easily. Avoid days that are too dry or wet as you will do more harm than good.

Replacing a tooth

Old-fashioned cultivating rakes have individual teeth that are whittled from wood. Using the rake when soil is moist and workable will reduce the chance of a tooth falling out.

RAKE STYLE

The width of the rake can vary considerably, with the number of teeth on the head usually ranging from 10 to 16. The greater the number of teeth, the finer the soil surface will be after raking. The most common garden rake has a flat head and either flat or slightly curved tines. It will do for most tasks with the exception of major grading or landscaping, which will necessitate a proper wooden grading rake.

After use, wash the rake thoroughly and dry it before storing. Wipe the head regularly with an oily cloth to prevent rust, and check that no teeth are working loose. Hang it in a dry place – preferably on the wall – so that the head cannot be trodden on.

CULTIVATORS

The traditional cultivator does not look much like a hoe, but plays a very similar role in the garden. It is designed to cultivate the upper layer of soil, break through surface compaction, and disturb weed seedlings. It usually has a long handle, and a head with between three and seven tines. Unlike the fork,

the tines are bent into sharply pointed hooks so that you can pull the tool through the soil in short, sharp movements like the draw hoe. The tines are flexible to absorb impact and staggered, like a clawed hand, so that you can make the equivalent of two pulls with just the one. Tine number, width, depth and shape varies according to the intended use.

STYLES OF CULTIVATOR

There are many versions of the cultivator that vary distinctly from the traditional, straight-handled tool with three to seven tines. Some have short handles with a T-shaped top bar and plastic polypropylene hand grips. Others have four tines (like a fork) that are staggered, instead of flat.

Hook cultivators should be pushed vertically down into the soil with the sole of the foot and given a twist to loosen the soil to the depth of the tines. This tool is useful in a confined area, as it is operated from an upright position rather than at an angle. Use it to incorporate fertilizer, loosen weeds, aid water absorption and reduce compaction. Where the plants are closely spaced, however, this type of cultivation may damage the roots by going too deep.

Dig deeply

Hook-like cultivators (left and above) break up the top layer of soil, relieving compaction, improving aeration and allowing rainwater to filter down to the subsoil. These tools are especially useful in established borders.

For planting bulbs and annuals, weeding your borders and transplanting rows of seedlings, a hand fork and trowel are indispensable. They are likely to be the tools that you use most often, so invest in good-quality products that will last for years to come.

HAND TOOLS

While the heavier work in the garden is done with long-handled tools, the more detailed, close-up work, such as weeding, tends to be finished off using hand tools. Their smaller size allows you to work nearer to the plants without causing as much potential damage to the stems and roots of those plants that you are weeding around.

In the garden, close cultivation means getting down to ground level and, if you are working for any significant length of time, you will be kinder to your knees and back if you sit, rather than kneel or bend over as you work. It can be very therapeutic, on a warm summer's afternoon, to sit and work methodically through a border, just letting your mind wander where it will as you get rid of unwanted weed seedlings and dead leaves.

Basic tool kit

Like so many implements, there seems to be a huge variety of hand tools, but you will only need a basic trowel and fork to start off with. Depending upon the size of your garden, this may be all you'll ever need,

but if you branch into growing vegetables you may find a use for specialized tools such as the onion hoe, which is good for earthing up onions and other plants.

Joints

Although the less expensive tools are pressed and shaped from a single piece of metal, those with wooden (ash) handles usually have a tang-and-ferrule joint. The tang is a sharp, spear-like point at the top of the metal head which fits into the end of the shaft, and is clamped into place with a ferrule (a small ring of steel) to stop the wood splitting. With a great deal of use, the tang will hit against the wood of the handle and create a space until it falls out. Generally, the more you pay for the tools, the better the ferrule will fit against the handle and the longer the tool will last.

What to look for

Most hand trowels and forks show little variation in basic design but vary considerably in terms of quality and cost. You should base your selection of any smaller hand tools on both sturdiness and comfort, as a smooth, well-made handle will reduce the risk of

Vegetable grower's tools

Eaten within a few hours of harvesting, home-grown vegetables are extremely good for you. Tasty and richer in vitamins than shop-bought produce, they are worth a little cosseting and a few special tools.

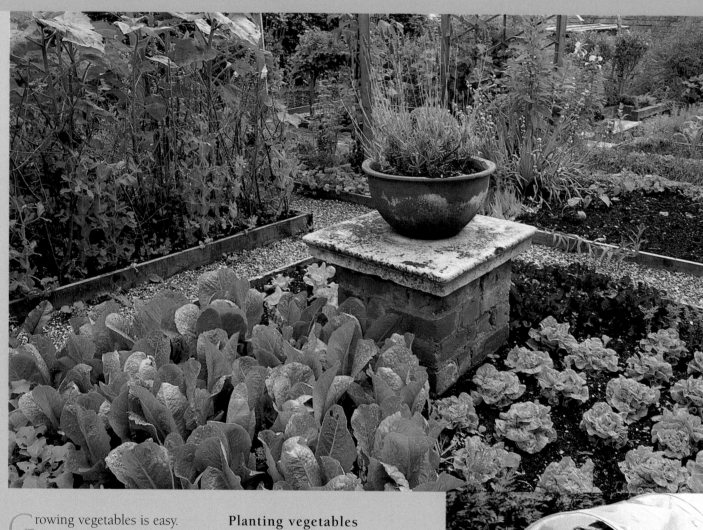

Growing vegetables is easy. Simply stick to four basic rules: site crops in full sun (they hate shade), rotate crops so that the big three (brassicas, root crops and all other vegetables) are never on the same patch for more than one year in three, and enrich the soil with bulky manure and well-rotted garden compost. The fourth rule is to use the right tools for the job.

Planting vegetables

After preparing the ground, the first step to new life in the vegetable plot is sowing seed. By all means pinch seeds between your finger and thumb and trickle them into a seed drill, but for more precision, try a dispenser calibrated for six different sizes of seed. A dibber is one of the most useful tools for a vegetable gardener. This slender cone of wood or metal, which may have depth indicators, is essential for planting cabbages, cauliflowers, brussels sprouts, kale and leeks. When putting in brassicas, make a hole with a dibber and insert the roots and lower part of the stem. Firm in the plant by making a second hole next to the first and levering soil against the stem.

A garden line is necessary for marking rows when sowing or planting. This consists of two 50-cm lengths of metal, one of which has a rotating holder around which 15 metres of jute twine is wound or unwound. If the string gets wet, unwind and dry, before re-winding it.

If you need something to stand on to sow or plant, you could use a board, but it's easier to unroll a path. Made from inter-locking heavy-duty polypropylene slats, a portable path can stretch to any length you choose.

Protecting your crop
You may need a tunnel cloche to warm and dry soil to sow lettuce, carrots, turnips and other crops in

Protective measures
Polythene cloches (left) form a complete barrier retaining moisture and air, whilst creating a warm, humid environment.

the spring. A strip of UV-stabilized polythene is draped over and secured to wire hoops, and can be erected quickly and easily. Some have built-in, galvanized steel hoops to make a one-piece tunnel.

Ornamental and practical, a rhubarb forcing pot is a large, lidded pot made from terracotta. Speed an early crop of tender pink stems by heaping leaves or straw over a dormant crown in winter. Enclose this with a forcing pot. Periodically, remove the lid to see how long shoots are. When they're just under the lid, remove the pot and enjoy eating the crop.

Harvesting vegetables
The asparagus knife, with its serrated blade, is ideal for cropping fleshy spears. The new shoots, about 13 cm long, are cut 8 cm below the soil. You could sever them with a normal knife, but it's tedious if you have a lot to do.

The long-handled draw hoe and the onion hoe will both come in handy. The former has a swan neck and a thin rectangular blade, the tip of which is angled to brush a taut garden line, to take out seed drills. Use it, too, for earthing-up trench celery and potatoes. The onion hoe is great to thin seedlings and weed around closely spaced crops. It has a swan neck, wooden handle and a hemispherical blade.

Choose a trowel that you find comfortable to hold, with a handle anchored firmly in place by a tang-and-ferrule design. The joint with the blade should also be strongly forged.

A deep dish and sharp blade lets you dig easily. Match the shape of the blade to the job in hand: if you are working in tight spaces or planting out seedlings and bulbs, a narrow and pointed blade will be helpful; for other digging tasks, a broader blade is preferable.

TROWELS

The trowel is used like a miniature spade or hoe in the garden, to dig small holes, transplant seedlings and small plants, turn over the surface of the soil and loosen weeds. It has a short handle and a dished head with a rounded end, ideal for moving small quantities of soil, compost or fertilizer around. A trowel enables you to work in a space as confined as a window box – where it is probably the only tool you will need until you branch out further.

Find a trowel best suited to your use. The more confined the space, or the smaller the plants you are handling, the narrower the trowel should be. After use, wash it thoroughly to remove any soil and allow it to dry completely before putting it away. Wipe it regularly with an oily cloth to prevent rust.

HAND FORKS

Just as the trowel is a miniature spade, so the hand fork is a small version of its much larger cousin, the border fork. A hand fork is useful for close-work in a border or container, particularly for breaking up the surface of the soil to allow rainwater to penetrate, for weeding and cultivating and for mixing in a top-dressing of fertilizer.

The hand fork may have flat or round tines (the flat-tined designs are better for weeding), allowing access to confined spaces and closely established plants. Choose the hand fork that best suits your needs, in terms of hand size and material. However, there is no

fatigue (caused by vibration as you work through the soil) and blisters. The handle may be made of ash (with or without a rubber handgrip), polypropylene, or aluminium (with head and handle cast as one unit). In some ranges, wooden handles are available in two lengths: 127 mm or 305 mm.

The head is usually metal, often carbon steel, although stainless-steel heads are available. A smooth surface on the blades or tines makes using and cleaning them much easier, and for this reason, carbon steel models tend to be coated with rust- and scratch-resistant paint.

Small-scale hand tools

Short-handled tools including trowel, hand fork and onion hoe are ideal for gardeners with a collection of containers or a few raised beds. The shorter the handle, the nearer to the action you place yourself and the more precise your movements.

point in spending a lot of money on a stainless-steel hand fork if it is not a tool that you intend to use often. Yet, a stainless-steel tool will last you a gardening lifetime.

ONION HOE

The onion hoe is a short-handled tool, designed like a small draw hoe. Use it in the vegetable garden for earthing-up (pulling soil up around the crop to blanch it or encourage growth) or pulling soil away to expose the crop to allow it to ripen, like the onion in late summer. Keep it low to the ground during use. It is small enough to use between closely planted crops, and can be used for weeding in a general way in flower borders and the vegetable plot.

THREE-PRONGED CULTIVATOR

This scaled-down version of the long-handled cultivator allows you to aerate the soil in a confined or small area, such as a raised bed, where a full-sized implement wouldn't work. The three curved or bent tines have pointed or flattened tips to scratch through the surface and loosen it.

> tools of the **future**

Don't damage your back doing the hard work in the garden. Shop around for tools with comfortable handles that reduce the strain. There are more around each season and an increasing interest in our health means that this is a trend that is likely to continue.

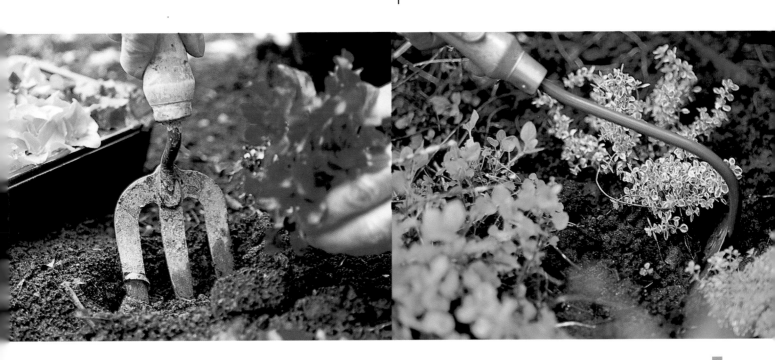

3

Controlling
the Environment

Watering wisely

Water is critical to the existence of plants. It's true that they need nutrients and light to thrive, but they need water just to survive. A plant may consist of as much as 90 per cent water, which is responsible for all the plant's basic functions. Moisture around the roots allows nutrients and minerals in the soil to be absorbed, while within the plant, water keeps the cells firm and allows the movement of the starches and sugars needed for growth. Moisture also triggers the swelling of seeds and their germination.

Without water, a plant's activities are severely limited: insufficient water can result in the shedding of buds; the premature drop of flowers; and poor colour and size in the flowers that do open. It can also cause premature leaf loss or early autumn colour; the production of few or small fruits; and an increased susceptibility to attack from pests and diseases.

WHAT CAUSES WILTING?

A lack of moisture in the soil forces plants to use up the water supplies held within their tissues. Once the amount of water lost from the leaves exceeds that taken in by the roots, the plant will start to draw moisture from its own cells. As this happens, the cells shrink, each losing contact with its neighbour, causing the loss of stability that we see as wilting. Restoring the supply of moisture in time allows the cells to refill and the plant to recover. If the wilting goes too far, however, the cells cannot refill and the plant will die. The stage at which it is impossible to reclaim the plant is known as the 'permanent wilting point'.

When rainfall is low, a plant growing in the soil can send its roots deeper into the soil to find reserves of water trapped in the lower layers of subsoil. This is not the case, however, for plants that you are growing in containers. These don't have a reservoir of moisture which their roots can draw on, and therefore rely on you for their watering needs – which may become time-consuming.

Exactly how much water a plant requires depends on the type and size of plant, and the conditions around it. Water is lost from the plant through tiny pores on the underside of the leaf, in a process known as transpiration. On a cool, calm day, transpiration

> **'Gardening requires lots of water – most of it in the form of perspiration.'**
>
> LOU ERICKSON, CRITIC AND POET (1840–1921)

will be minimal, but on a windier day, moisture is constantly evaporating and being replaced from within the plant at a faster rate – so the plant's needs are greater. On a really warm, windy day, the loss is at its highest, and the plant will use up a great deal of water. You may need to refresh container-grown plants twice on a hot day – particularly if they are leafy like tomato plants.

HUMIDITY AND WATER LOSS

The humidity of the air surrounding the plant also influences its rate of moisture loss. The more moisture there is in the air, the less water the plant will lose, as the pressure within the leaf will be closer to that outside it. This applies particularly to house plants: the air indoors tends to be dry – especially in winter – when heating and fires have a marked drying effect on the air.

The simplest method of increasing the humidity around a plant is to stand it on a wide saucer of pebbles and keep the saucer replenished with water. The roots will have access to a constant supply of water without actually standing in it (and potentially rotting) and the water can evaporate around the leaves of the plant, reducing the moisture lost. Grouping plants together also helps, as the canopy of leaves creates a microclimate underneath that raises the humidity level.

TIME TO WATER

Water your plants in the early morning and late evening, when the soil is cool and the atmosphere is relatively moist, as this will allow the maximum time for water to soak in before the heat of the next day. Watering when it's hot not only guarantees maximum evaporation, but also increases the danger of droplets on the leaves causing scorch.

Watering your plants can be extremely therapeutic, especially at the end of a stressful day when you can let your mind wander and your body relax. Through it you will get to know your plants and how much water each requires, while checking their health. If you are regularly away from home, however, you should try an automatic watering system. It operates a timer and switches on at a specified time to deliver a pre-set quantity of water.

Water therapy

Take the chore out of watering by investing in a water sprinkler (above). You can even watch from a comfortable garden seat (left).

WATERING EQUIPMENT

Plants like to be treated gently. Drowning them in a strong jet of water will damage delicate leaves and stems, and also wash away valuable soil; on the other hand, too fine a mist may deprive the roots of sufficient moisture. Good-quality watering tools should therefore allow you to deliver a steady and controllable stream of water.

WATERING CANS

A good-quality watering can is a must for any gardener. You need it for spot-watering thirsty plants, moistening seed trays and applying both liquid fertilizer and pesticide.

When buying a can for the first time, select a well-balanced one that is comfortable to carry when full and heavy. When filled, it should start to pour as soon as it is tilted. A can with a long spout will give you extra reach among the plants for individual watering. The volume of water the can will hold may be as little as half a litre – which is useful for just a few house plants – and as much as 16 litres.

Look for a can with a detachable rose or nozzle that fits onto the spout. By changing the shape and size of the rose, you can be sure of delivering the correct amount of water to your plants. If you plan to raise seedlings, choose a rose that provides a spray of water rather than a jet. If you apply a jet to a small plant you may wash it out of the soil and kill it, whereas a gentle shower will moisten it without harm.

Watering cans are generally made of plastic or galvanized steel. Plastic ones are cheaper, lighter and will last many years providing they are protected, as

>good ideas

If you never seem to have enough hands to carry everything you need around your garden, consider a watering can with side pockets for your hand tools. This model also has a domed half-lid to stop water from spilling out, and two handles which will help you tip the can when full.

weathering may cause them to degrade. Metal cans are more expensive and heavier, but will last indefinitely if cared for; rapid repairs to any rust will prolong its life.

MISTERS

These are hand-held containers with a trigger that you squeeze to release a fine, mist spray. They hold from a half to a full litre of liquid and are ideal for increasing

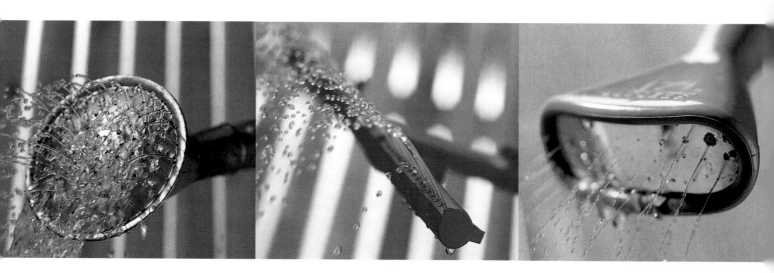

the humidity around smaller plants in the house or greenhouse. Buy a second and third mister to apply small amounts of foliar feed or pesticide – but keep these labelled and separate to avoid contamination.

Misters are small and inexpensive, made of plastic and will last for many seasons. As with any plastic items, it is a good idea to store them out of direct sunlight to stop the material from perishing.

THE GARDEN HOSE

The hose will form the basis of your watering system once you progress beyond a single can. It takes the effort out of watering, saving you the back-breaking effort of carrying water from tap to plants. The hose will deliver a constant stream of water and can be pulled around the garden to reach every plant.

Lawns need watering only when browning signs of water stress become visible. Then it will take around 25 litres per square metre to restore it. This volume is difficult to deliver without a hose, but more importantly, in dry conditions it is more effective to soak the grass via a slow-running hose than to use a lawn sprinkler. The frequent light applications of water produced by a sprinkler encourage shallow rooting, making the grass vulnerable if watering is discontinued and therefore less self-sufficient.

Hoses are made of vinyl, nylon or polythene but they vary in quality, cost and durability. The cheaper ones consist of a single layer of material; the more expensive ones have an inner tube coated in vinyl or a woven nylon mesh coated in vinyl (or a vinyl-rubber mixture). The latter are better for working at higher water pressures and are designed to resist kinking and degradation. Hoses are available in different colours, including green, brown, black, red and sand, to blend or contrast with your garden.

Connectors These are useful for times when you need to join the hose to another item; if your garden is long or the tap in an inaccessible place, it may be necessary to join lengths of hose together. You may wish to

THE LOWDOWN ON HOSING DOWN

You may think a hose is a simple piece of equipment, but in fact a lot of thought goes into making a good hose. Look for brands made from several different layers or plies of material, which strengthen the hose and help to prevent kinking. To prolong the life of your hose, keep it properly coiled and out of direct sunlight (which will cause it to deteriorate).

change from one type of watering device to another, such as the sprinkler to the hand pistol. Interchangeable fittings with snap-on couplings make this a convenient option.

Connectors are often made of brightly coloured plastic that is easily visible in the garden, and each simply joins to the next by pushing together. Brass fittings offer a more permanent (although more expensive) system that will last a lifetime.

You can find fittings that will connect to the tap (whatever shape it is); fit to the end of a hose ready to connect to another item; double the hose to feed two separate hoses; lengthen the hose by joining two together; and repair a split hose. They simply attach to the hose by a screw fitting, with rubber O-rings or circular springs to ensure a watertight fit.

Lances and pistols These are devices for delivering water and fit to the end of a hose with a connector. Pistols usually allow you to adjust the delivery from a fine spray to a direct jet to suit the plants being watered, and include an on/off position for when you pause to examine a plant while watering. They can be plastic or brass (with a polypropylene grip). Lances come in brass or lighter-weight aluminium, with a moulded grip, and provide an extension to the hose for reaching inaccessible plant containers, such as hanging baskets, to deliver a fine spray.

Watering roses

A round rose (left) delivers a gentle spray; long-handled extensions (middle) allow you to water out-of-reach containers and beds; oval roses (right) deliver a stronger spray, ideal for your more robust plants.

Fruit-growing tools

Sun-ripened apples and pears straight from the bough are a perk of growing fruit in your back garden. You can also enjoy a foam of blossom in the spring, and a wealth of delicious puddings and pies are yours to make for next to nothing.

To make your fruit bush or tree more productive and to keep it within bounds, you will need to prune it. A conventional pair of secateurs or loppers is usually adequate (see pages 68–71), but if you have weak wrists, seek out ratchet, double-lever or geared secateurs and loppers that easily slice through shoots and branches.

Some apple varieties grow so much each season that it is easier to prune them with a pull-action saw designed to cut green, sappy wood without clogging. Choose a folding version with a high-carbon, hard chrome-plated blade with specially set teeth that leave a knife-cut finish.

You'll need a pruning knife to pare ragged saw cuts and take off snags and side shoots (page 72) and long-arm pruners will be invaluable for reaching shoots up to 4.5 metres from the ground. The last pruning tool you may need is a pair of vine scissors – ideal for snipping out shoots without damaging fruits; for thinning grapes and spacing apple, pear and plum fruitlets.

Protecting your crop
Fruit cages are a good investment against bud-pecking and fruit-stealing birds. Don't stint on size as you will regret it if you wish to increase your plantings and you

For delicate tasks

If you enjoy grafting fruit trees, a budding knife (left) will come in handy. Long and slender, with a serrated blade, vine scissors (below) are perfect for the fine work of thinning grapes.

For out-of-reach branches

A telescopic pole that you can fit with different heads, such as loppers (above) or a fruit picker (above right), is invaluable. When using a fruit picker, ease the metal 'fingers' fringing the bag around a fruit and give it gentle tug to detach it.

haven't room for them. A cage should also be about 2 metres in height as it's no fun having to bend low to pick the fruit.

Essentially, a cage comprises a galvanized or black plastic-coated steel frame draped with 2–3 cm mesh netting – usually made of polypropylene. You can use galvanized zinc wire for the sides of the cage but not the roof, as zinc can dissolve in the rain and is toxic

to plants. There should also be one or more doors with a 'spade-end' hinge to prevent twisting.

Tree ties

Some trees, especially apples grafted onto dwarfing M27 rootstock, need supporting throughout their life. Do this by securing the trunk with an adjustable buckle tie, which prevents the bark from chafing, to a short stake which has been pressure-treated with preservative to keep it rot-free.

Harvesting your fruit

The best part of a growing an apple, pear or plum tree is eating the ripened fruit: but it has to be picked first. It's vital not to bruise it, so handle with care.

If you can reach the fruits from the ground or with a stepladder or ladder tethered to a branch, pack them gently, one by one, into a

foam-lined bucket or wicker basket. Alternatively, consign them to a canvas or strong nylon bag with handles. The best are self-supporting for filling and emptying, but easily collapsed for carrying and storing.

The finest fruits, however, are usually clustered on branch tips, often out of reach. The solution is to harvest the crop with a purpose-made fruit picker. Tools for picking fruit have a strong, fabric bag attached to a crown of plastic or galvanized prongs or fingers. Some have an adjustable, angled head. Whichever you use, connect it to a lightweight, telescopic handle that allows you to pick fruits up to 5 metres from the ground. Simply manoeuvre the fruit stalk between the pair of prongs and tug gently. The fruit will drop into the bag. Gather one fruit at a time to avoid bruising.

Non-return valves Fit a non-return (double-check) valve into your watering system between the mains supply and the hose to prevent contamination of the supply through back-siphoning. This is particularly important if you add a liquid fertilizer to the water as you are applying it to the plants.

Hose reels Made of metal or polypropylene, a reel is a convenient device for keeping hoses tidy, rather than unravelled and unsafe on the floor. You can carry it, mount it on the wall or wheel it around the garden, unwinding just the length of hose you need to reach the plant you want to water. Some models may have a guide that encourages the hose to run smoothly, and most have a winding handle or knob on the side to rewind the hose onto the central drum.

Hose guides and finials These protect border plants from possible damage as you drag the hose around the garden. Ornamental or retractable, each has a rotating reel on a vertical spike with which you anchor the guide into the ground. The retractable type is ideal for the lawn: pull it up for use and push down again for easy mowing. Wall-mounted types prevent the hose chafing against the wall as it is used.

Diluters A through-hose diluter allows you to apply liquid fertilizer at the same time as watering. These relatively inexpensive devices release fertilizer into the water at an adjustable rate. They can be free-standing units for the larger garden, or smaller jug-shaped attachments near the hand grip. Each can be used with a lance or pistol-grip delivery system.

DRIP-FEED SYSTEMS

Using a hose can be a hit-and-miss affair unless you have perfected your technique. A more accurate system involves delivering water to individual plants, which reduces the amount of water lost by evaporation and weeds between the plants. There are two sorts of perforated hose to do this: one is flat with perforations on one side, which send out a fine spray over a 2-metre wide strip. The other is a rigid, circular

Lightening the burden

Make life easier for yourself by investing in a wall-mounted hose reel, which rewinds automatically (left). Or, dispense with watering duties altogether and opt for an automatic drip-feed system (below).

hose with perforations around and along its length allowing water to seep out at a very low pressure directly into the soil.

Both perforated hoses are laid on the soil's surface and are good for irrigating large areas. The water soaks right down into the soil, encouraging plant roots to penetrate deeply. These pipes are quite often left in position permanently.

Both drip-feed systems can easily be automated, as the flow of water is slow and unlikely to overwhelm the plants. The timer may be electric or battery-driven and can be set to deliver the water when it will be most beneficial to the plants, such as the late evening. It can be set up to run every day of the summer or for short periods when you are on holiday. It is ideal if you work erratic hours or are likely to forget to water. The run time is adjustable, from one minute to two hours, with a frequency from once an hour to once a week, as you see fit.

Container watering Spaghetti tubing consists of a main supply pipe, connected to fine pipes leading directly to each plant or container. These can be adjusted to deliver a steady, fine trickle of water or drips, and are held in place on plastic clips. However, the fine gauge of the tubing means that this type of

Watering your lawn

The spike sprinkler (left) delivers a circular pattern of water, ideal for small areas; rotating sprinklers (centre) give larger coverage; while oscillating ones (right) are perfect for rectangular and square lawns.

system has a tendency to clog in hard water areas (with large amounts of free lime in the water), or if soluble plant foods are applied during watering.

SPRINKLERS

These fit onto the end of a hose and anchor into the ground, delivering a spray of droplets over a wide area. They are useful for watering a newly laid lawn to settle it in, but can be rather wasteful for any serious watering, as much of the water evaporates rather than penetrating down into the lower layers of the soil. This encourages shallow-rooting and makes the plants more susceptible to drought.

Static sprinklers These consist of a spike which you press into the ground, and a nozzle that delivers the water in a circular pattern over a given area.

Rotary-hammer sprinklers Ideal for small areas, these are based on a nozzle and counter-balance mechanism, which works to move the water jet in a series of short, swinging motions.

Oscillating sprinklers These have a central spray bar with a series of holes in the top and sides. On the side of the bar is a drive mechanism, operated by water pressure, which moves the bar from side to side. The speed of oscillation is dependent on the water pressure. Many models are adjustable so the water covers different sized areas.

Mobile sprinklers Connecting to the hose, these will travel over an area or planned route to water a larger area, such as a lawn. The front wheel follows the hose reel and the rotation of the arms drives the forward momentum, so that the speed at which the sprinkler travels is dictated by the water pressure. The lower the pressure, the slower the speed.

Rotary sprinklers These have a number of nozzles on a central pivot which rotates in a circular motion. Water coverage is usually even, and the rotary speed is governed by the water pressure.

SPRAYERS

These may be hand-held, self-standing or worn on the back during use. They are used chiefly to apply chemicals such as herbicides and pesticides, so if you garden organically, you may need one only for applying foliar feeds.

On manual types, you operate a pump handle which builds up the pressure inside the container in order to deliver the liquid. Control the rate of application by adjusting the delivery nozzle (which is usually at the end of a short lance) or the operating pressure of the carrying vessel. Remember to wash the sprayer thoroughly after each use, so that there is no chance of cross-contamination of chemicals.

A typical cordless, rechargeable, electric sprayer will give two hours continuous use from a single charge. Like the manual type, it has an adjustable nozzle, providing a cone or fan distribution pattern.

BUTTS

Use a water butt for short-term storage of water, and collect rainwater via a gutter or drainpipe, as this will be much less alkaline than treated water. Most butts

> **tools of the future**

Watering a large area can mean that you are endlessly bending over to pick the hose up and move it around the garden with you. This innovative hose trolley will put an end to tiring bending and also keep your hands clean: pull the handle and the hose will be cleanly laid out, and push it to roll up the hose.

are fitted with a tap and hose connector at the base so that you can fill your watering can. Cover the top of the water butt to exclude light and reduce the growth of algae in the water.

If you have a big garden or a vast vegetable patch, a large plastic barrel holding 180–230 litres will be needed, though smaller barrels are available, holding just 100 litres. A slim, rectangular, wall-mounted butt will fit snugly around the drainpipe and hold 115 litres. A built-in diverter will prevent it overflowing.

Spraying trees

This has always seemed to involve either leaning precariously from a ladder or dodging the falling spray if you reach up from below. Now you can get a small, pressurized sprayer with a flexible hose extension to give you an extra 2.5-metre reach. So, you can stand comfortably on the ladder and simply reach out over the tree.

Reading the weather

After you have been gardening for a while, you will begin to read the weather and recognize its changes. This will have a bearing on what actions you take for the plants in your care. If the day is going to be hot, then the greenhouse should be ventilated and shaded, and your plants will need watering at least once. If it is going to be windy, taller plants might need protection, and in cold, wet conditions, you may have to move small seedlings indoors.

If you keep a record of the weather on a regular basis you can look back and compare one year with another to see when plants flowered or cropped. This is not an arduous task and can be achieved by setting up your own small weather station to record the prevailing conditions.

WEATHER STATIONS

The most accurate readings are obtained when the instruments taking the measurements are in the ideal position. Your rain gauge should be outside so that it can catch the rain and the wind-speed recorder should obviously be in an exposed position to catch the wind, but the thermometer needs shelter from bright sunlight and hostile elements. The traditional weather station, a Stevenson screen, is a free-standing, four-sided box on legs, with louvred sides rather than solid wood. Few gardens today would have room for such a large case, but it is possible to buy or make a wall-mounted version with a screen front to house your thermometer.

RAIN GAUGES

Essentially a calibrated container, the rain gauge is designed to catch and measure a representative sample of the rainfall in your garden. Its accuracy depends on where it is positioned in the garden, and ideally it should be placed a third of a metre above the ground and well away from overhanging obstructions such as trees, hedges and buildings. It can also be used to measure the amount of water distributed by a lawn sprinkler, by positioning it on the grass about halfway between the sprinkler unit and the outer edge of the watering pattern. Watering to a depth of 1 cm twice a week (loamy soil) or three times a week (sandy soil) is adequate for good lawn growth.

All-in-one weather station

For a modest outlay, you can get a compact weather station (left) which stakes into the ground and monitors rainfall, wind speed and direction, and temperature. Most rain gauges measure rainfall in mm and inches (below).

WEATHER STATIONS | 49

SUNDIALS THROUGH THE AGES

A sundial is a device that measures the time. There are many different types, but most consist of a stationary stick or arm, known as a gnomon, that casts a shadow onto a plate or surface marked with the hours; as the sun moves through the sky, the shadow rotates across the plate.

The Egyptians used a form of sundial as early as 1500 BC. This consisted of a tall stone obelisk, which cast a shadow onto the ground; markers arranged on the ground indicated the time and identified the longest and shortest days of the year. Later, a more accurate sundial was developed, using the gnomon and plate system described above. Cultures as diverse as the Greeks, Romans, Arabs and Chinese depended on these finely crafted instruments, and different forms evolved, including horizontal, vertical and tilted models. By the 18th century, however, clocks and watches began to supersede sundials, and today they are mostly prized for ornamental purposes.

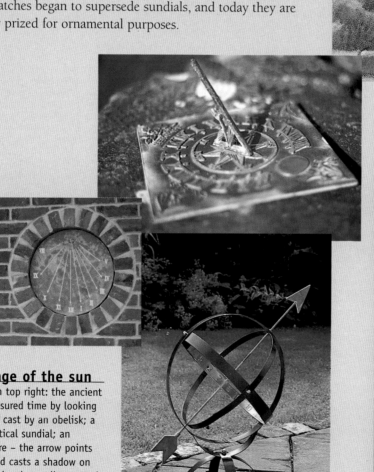

The passage of the sun
Clockwise from top right: the ancient Egyptians measured time by looking at the shadow cast by an obelisk; a decorative vertical sundial; an armillary sphere – the arrow points polar north and casts a shadow on the equatorial band; a wall-mounted vertical sundial; a horizontal sundial of the sort commonly mounted on pedestals in gardens.

Rain gauges can be as simple as a calibrated funnel standing in a container. The less expensive ones may not be frostproof, and if a frost occurs while the container is holding water, then the resultant expansion will crack it. The newest ones are moulded from styrene acrylonitrile, which is strong, clear and durable. They fit onto a broom handle driven vertically into the ground and have a scale on the side of the container for taking measurements. Readings should be taken daily and any water discarded.

WIND SPEED AND DIRECTION INDICATORS

To measure the speed and force of the wind, you need a small anemometer. This consists of three metal cups, turned on their sides and fixed to a vertical spindle by arms which rotate when blown by the wind. The wind speed is calculated in knots from the number of rotations recorded on the meter in a certain period.

The direction of the wind can be registered using a weather vane mounted on a building or garden structure. This is a freely rotating, horizontal arm with a vertical, flat surface at one end and a pointer at the other. Knowing the prevailing direction will influence where you site certain structures in your garden, and knowing the speeds will help you plan when to begin planting and whether to ventilate your greenhouse.

THERMOMETERS

Knowing the temperature around your plants allows you to decide when to ventilate, water and protect them from frost. In the greenhouse, a sharp rise in temperature will cause stress to the plants, their rate of transpiration will increase and the resultant loss of water may cause wilting.

Position your thermometer out of direct sunlight and the elements (rain, snow and wind) so that the read-out is representative of the general position. This may mean attaching it to a wall, and some models are available for wall-mounting. Many thermometers give readings for both the maximum day temperature and

Taking the temperature

Thermometers range from the traditional mercury types (left) to digital versions (centre). Some models attach to the surround of a window frame (right), enabling you to take a reading without leaving the warmth of your home.

the minimum night-time temperature, so that you can see if a frost is imminent and the plants need protection. Garden thermometers give readings in both Celsius and Fahrenheit and will last many years as long as they are not damaged.

HYGROMETERS

These devices measure the humidity of the atmosphere. In many cases, a digital thermometer will give a humidity reading as well, which allows you to decide whether the moisture levels in the air around your plants are adequate. You can then decide whether you need to damp down the floor to increase the level or ventilate to lower it. Traditional hygrometers operate using human hair (or a synthetic replacement for it) on a hair-spring movement.

BAROMETERS

Changes in the weather are heralded by a change in atmospheric pressure. A barometer will record these changes and give you advance warning of what is to come. A steady rise in pressure usually indicates good weather to come, and a rapid fall, bad. There are two types of barometer, mercury and aneroid (or dry). The latter are portable and cheaper.

Greenhouse tools

Conservatories and greenhouses are apt to get very hot in the summer and cold in the winter, so you will probably need to take steps to create a balanced growing environment for your plants.

RESERVOIRS

A mains reservoir will stabilize the flow of water for a drip-feed system, steadying and reducing it to provide a continuous supply at a suitable rate. A plastic case and aluminium lid make it ideal for the greenhouse.

A 2-litre capacity plastic water reservoir can be attached to the side or end of the benching in the greenhouse. It has an aluminium lid to exclude light and prevent the growth of algae, and will hold enough water to supply capillary matting laid along the bench to keep the plants standing on it moist. The automated version is connected to a water supply and has a ball valve to start and stop the flow. The supply may be the mains, a water butt or an overhead tank.

CAPILLARY MATTING

This is a coarse, loosely woven, cotton-polyester material designed to allow free movement of water over a flat, level surface. Use it to cover your bench before laying your pots out, and it will act as a wick, drawing water from a reservoir for distribution to the plants. Ensure good contact between the matting and the compost in the pot, so the water can be sucked up by the capillary action of the compost and used by the roots. If the pots have been 'crocked' with pieces of broken terracotta, the system won't work.

SELF-WATERING TRAYS

Each consists of a watertight plastic base tray (the reservoir) and an aluminium insert which holds a layer of capillary matting. The matting draws water up from the reservoir for the plants. There should be enough water for two weeks' supply – while you are away on holiday, for instance. They are available in a wide range of sizes and colours.

GREENHOUSE SHADING

In summer, the heat inside the greenhouse, especially at midday, can be intense. This will increase the rate of transpiration of the plants, leading to wilting, and more directly, it can scorch the leaves by literally cooking the cells on the leaf surface.

You can buy blinds which you attach to either side of the greenhouse windows. External woven plastic ones are supplied on a roll with a pulley bracket and strong nylon thread to allow them to be pulled up or down. They will give partial or total coverage, according to weather conditions, and will last for

Adequate ventilation

Introduce a much-needed breeze to the greenhouse during the hot summer months with adjustable slats (right), which you open by hand, or install automatic vent openers (far right).

Heating and cooling

A portable electric fan heater (far left) is one of the easiest ways to keep your greenhouse warm during winter. If you prefer not to install blinds in the summer, reduce and diffuse the sunlight by painting whitewash or diluted emulsion onto the outside of the glass or plastic (left).

many years, especially if you store them indoors over winter. Woven green shade netting can be used inside or out, and has a four- to five-year life expectancy. Its pre-woven slits allow you to anchor it to the roof.

Inside the greenhouse, polyester roller blinds with non-rust aluminum rollers will last at least five years. The same fabric, bought loose, can be laid in the roof supports of a larger greenhouse and drawn across as required. Dot matrix shading film is self-adhesive (by static electricity) to flat glass or polycarbonate panels, although it will not stick to heavy corrugations. It may also be used outside, but will not last as long.

INSULATION

During winter, you can greatly reduce the amount of heat lost from inside your greenhouse by insulating it. This helps to keep the greenhouse frost-free and allows you to sustain plants without the cost of a heater. The simplest form of insulation is bubble polythene which has two layers of clear polythene welded together into layers of bubbles, producing a triple-glazed effect. You can buy it on a roll, cut it to length and attach it to the inside of your greenhouse frame with plastic clips. Remove and store it once the danger of frost has passed.

HEATERS

The two main benefits of greenhouse heating are that you can keep tender plants alive in winter and sow seed for new plants early in the season. These new plants will be ready to go outside as soon as the weather warms up. You have several options:

Electric heaters With variable thermostatic controls, electric fan heaters can be used without heat as fans during the summer to circulate air and cool the greenhouse. They can be free-standing or wall-mounted. Hot-air blowers can be free-standing or hung from the roof. Air is drawn over an electric-powered, heating element. Designed for wall-mounting, electric convector heaters operate almost silently. Position them so that air can flow freely through both top and bottom.

Gas heaters The fuel can be propane or natural gas. Their thermostats may incorporate a safety cut-out carbon dioxide sensor which operates when the level of oxygen falls too low for healthy plant growth.

Paraffin heaters These range from very small heaters intended to keep the temperature barely above freezing to larger ones that can maintain a much higher temperature or heat a larger space. They are cheap to run and give off small amounts of carbon dioxide which is used by the plants to grow.

AUTOMATIC VENT OPENERS

Ideally, a greenhouse should have a ventilation area equal to a fifth of the floor area, and this should include louvred vents in the sides as well as opening roof panels. Automatic vent openers (for the roof or side panels) are ideal if you are out during the day or are unable to act if the temperature rises quickly. They operate using an enclosed cylinder of wax, which expands with heat to push a piston, which in turn causes the vent to open. As the wax cools, it contracts and a spring closes the vent again. You can preset the temperature at which they open to suit your plants. Some incorporate a hydraulic damper to prevent the window twisting if caught by a strong gust of wind.

4

Cutting
and Trimming

Lawncare

The lawn is an essential part of most gardens, providing a counterpoint to colourful borders. It acts much like the carpet does indoors, linking areas together throughout the garden, providing soft paths underfoot. You can use it as a soft surface on which to play games or simply sit to enjoy the sights and sounds of the garden. However, if you want to keep it in good condition (which requires hard work) it will occupy as much time in maintenance as any other aspect of your garden.

You can adapt the level of maintenance to suit the situation, because not everyone wants the same from their lawn or wants to put in the same effort. A beautiful, fine-leaved sward with mowing stripes will look perfect in an ornamental situation where there is little or no foot traffic, but where there are children, the grass will need to be much tougher to withstand a wide range of activities. If a wildflower meadow is your preferred option, you will need to cut the lawn once or twice a year to coincide with the flowering frequency of the plants growing through the grass.

Ornamental gardens

To keep a high-quality, formal lawn looking its best, use a cylinder mower with a roller, which will give the finest cut and create a banded effect (main picture). You will probably want to tidy the edges of your borders with a half-moon edging iron (inset).

Mowing is one of the routine, backbone tasks of gardening which makes all the difference to the health and appearance of your garden. While it is actively growing, your lawn may need mowing once a week to keep it looking good, but the benefits are not confined simply to shortening the length of the individual grass blades. By cutting and rolling them, you are encouraging the plant to 'tiller', or shoot again from the base. This results in a short, bushy plant which can withstand being walked on, rather than a single-leaved one which, if damaged, will die away and leave a bare patch.

Lawns are seldom made up of a single species of grass, as the finer ones which give the best-looking finish are not hard-wearing underfoot and benefit from the presence of tougher varieties to protect them. If the lawn is not cut regularly, then the stronger species will dominate the finer ones, resulting in a much coarser and more uneven finish.

CUTTING TIPS

Mowing is best undertaken when the grass is dry, so the clippings will be light and easy to deal with. Cutting wet grass will clog the mower blades so that you regularly have to stop to clear them, and also risks ripping the entire grass plant out of the soil rather than just cutting it. Allow the lawn to dry for at least 24 hours after heavy rain, as long as the ground beneath is not too wet. Morning dew can be swept off with a broom or a length of hose pipe to dry the lawn more quickly.

The golden rule of mowing is that you never remove more than one third of the total height of the grass in a single cut. Thus, set the blades high for the first cut of the year in the spring, and then reduce them in height as the season progresses.

SAFETY PRECAUTIONS FOR ALL MOWERS

- Use a residual current device (see page 128) for all mowers powered by mains electricity.
- Unplug before you make any adjustments.
- Never leave the machine with the motor running.
- Make sure the blades are securely attached.
- Wear sturdy footwear and trousers in case the mower goes over your foot or flicks out a stone.

The cylinder mower

This works by rotating a cylinder of metal blades (inset) as the mower is propelled across the lawn. Many models have grass boxes to collect the cuttings, which you can then transfer to your compost pile.

LAWN MOWERS

So many mowers are now available that the hardest part of maintaining a lawn can often be deciding which mower to buy! For optimum efficiency, choose a mower that suits the size and style of your lawn. If you have a large garden, for example, invest in a machine with a wide blade; for those with small lawns, a mower with narrow blades will be more suitable. Similarly, if your lawn has tight curves or corners, a smaller model will be easier to manoeuvre.

MOWER POWER

One of the first things you need to consider is how you wish to power your mower. There are four main options from which to choose.

Manual mowers are propelled by you. Cheap, quiet and with no awkward leads, these also provide a great aerobic workout for you! They are eco-friendly but

hard work to operate, particularly on slopes, so are probably most suitable for small gardens. They don't cope well with very long or wet grass. Some hand-push models have wheels at the sides, but these make it difficult to mow right up to the edges. Others are operated with a chain from a heavy roller at the back; this type of mower is easier to mow over edges and also creates attractive stripes on your lawn.

Electric-powered mowers are easier on the muscles, but their range is limited by the length of the lead. They tend to overheat when faced with long grass and tough jobs and for safety reasons should never be used on wet grass. If your lawn is very large or situated away from your home (and thus the power supply), these may not be the best option for you.

Petrol-driven mowers are the most powerful type, but also the most expensive and difficult to maintain. They are the best choice for large gardens as they can cover ground quickly and you don't have to worry about trailing cables. Opt for one with an electric ignition for ultimate ease of use: the pull-start models can be hard work to get going.

WHICH MOWER IS RIGHT FOR YOU?

	CYLINDER	ROTARY	RECIPROCATING KNIFE	FLAIL	NYLON-CORD TRIMMER
Rough grass/scrub			○	○	○
Uneven ground		○	○		○
Long grass		○	○	○	
Awkward space					○
Short grass	○	○	○		
Ornamental	○	○			

The rotary mower

Ideal for family lawns, rotary mowers are generally fitted with rear-mounted grassbags or boxes. The blade (inset) revolves at high speed, a bit like a helicopter, cutting through the grass as it goes.

Battery-powered mowers are not sufficiently powerful to tackle large gardens without needing to be recharged, but they are perfectly suitable for small and medium-sized gardens.

THE CUTTING EDGE

The next choice you need to make concerns the way the mower actually cuts the grass. First consider the type of lawn you have in your garden. Is it purely ornamental, or will the children be playing on it? The more ornamental the lawn, the finer the finish you will need from the mower, so you should be looking for one with a cutting cylinder rather than a rotary blade (see overleaf). Check that the handle is at the right height for you before you make a purchase and that the weight suits you. Bear in mind also that a good mower will last for years if you maintain it properly, so you are buying for yourself in perhaps ten years time as well as today.

>tools of the future

Mowing even a small lawn can be a chore, which is why some ingenious manufacturers have developed robotic lawn mowers that do all the work for you. The only preparation necessary is to install a sensor cable around the edge of the lawn. Then you simply press the 'on' switch and the mower will navigate its own way around the grass. When the machine approaches the cable, impact sensors redirect it. These sensors also keep it away from hard obstacles. There is no grass box, but regular trimming ensures that cuttings fall, shrivel and fertilize the lawn.

Some models are solar-powered; others have a battery that supplies the current and come with a special charging station in which the computer senses when the battery needs recharging and a guide wire directs the machine back to the charging station.

THE HISTORY OF LAWN MOWERS

Plans for the first lawn mower were patented in 1830 by an English engineer named Edwin Beard Budding. His machine consisted of a large rear roller and a front cutting cylinder, with gear wheels that transferred power from the roller to the cylinder. Over the next few decades, lighter, quieter machines were invented that used a chain or side wheels to drive the cylinder.

Steam and the more popular petrol-powered mowers were being manufactured at the end of the 19th century, and in the 1920s and 1930s electric and rotary cutting machines started to appear. The basic design of the domestic mower then changed remarkably little for years, until the hover mower was born in the early 1960s.

Lawncare solutions

Anticlockwise from top: a 19th-century cylinder mower with a front-mounted grass collection box; the permanently manicured lawn became an achievable dream in the 1950s and 1960s, thanks to cheaper and more efficient mowers; petrol, electric- and battery-powered machines made grass cutting even easier; the lightweight hover mower caught on quickly in the 1970s; today's ride-on models take the effort out of mowing and are enjoyable to use.

Some mowers leave the cut grass on the lawn; others come equipped with bags or boxes for collecting the clippings; and some actually recycle the clippings as they mow, cutting them down to a fine mulch, which is then left on the lawn to decompose and return nutrients to the grass.

Cylinder mowers Manual or powered, these give the best results, especially when cutting the finer grass species. They work thanks to their metal blades, which are arranged in a spiral on a cylinder and brush very closely against a fixed blade, cutting the grass in a scissor action. The number of blades varies from three to twelve – the greater the number, the finer the cut.

These mowers generally have a large rear roller, which flattens the grass and encourages 'tillering' (more shoots growing from the base of the plant), and a small front roller, which supports the front and allows you to adjust the cutting height.

After use, clean any clippings off the blades of the cylinder and wipe them clean with an oily cloth. Store the mower in a dry place. With average use, the blades will probably need sharpening every two years, but they can be tested by feeding a piece of newspaper between the blade and the sole plate.

Hand mowers The traditional hand-powered push mower makes the shush-shush sound so readily associated with the warm, sunny Sunday afternoons of childhood. It was a much less intrusive noise than the irritating, non-stop drone of today's electric models which invades the consciousness like the buzzing of a

Mower details

A height adjuster for the blades (left) allows you to control the cutting height. Rollers (centre) create a striped finish. This safety feature (right) will cut out the engine if you let go of the handle.

nearby wasp. The hand mower is ideal for small lawns, is an excellent form of exercise and is totally environmentally friendly.

This type of cylinder mower is usually fitted with a large, heavy, rear roller, which provides the drive for the machine via a chain or gear connection to the front cutting cylinder. In the hands of an experienced user it gives a wonderful striped effect.

Smaller models, often called reel mowers, are quick and easy to use and just have a cutting cylinder, driven by two side wheels, with or without a grass box to collect the cuttings.

Rotary mowers These machines are usually electric or petrol-powered. They have horizontally-set blades which rotate at high speed – around 3000 rpm – cutting as they spin. The number of blades varies from machine to machine, between two and four, and they may be triangular or rectangular.

The finish is not as good as that of the cylinder mower, but is ideal for play areas and 'useful' lawns. As the season progresses you can vary the height of the cut. Set the cutting height high at the beginning of the season, then lower it as desired, to produce

You can move the hover sideways as well as backwards and forwards, making it a good choice for gardens with awkward turns, banks, slopes and overhanging plants.

Hover mowers This type of rotary mower operates on a cushion of air without the need for wheels. A fan mounted on the engine draws air in through holes in the top of the cover, forcing it down to create the pressure that lifts the machine. Having no wheels makes this very manoeuvrable on steep slopes and uneven areas, and for cutting long or wet grass.

After use, remove any clippings which are stuck in the intake grill or on the blade(s) and wipe clean with an oily cloth. Store the mower in a dry place. With average use, the blades will probably need sharpening or replacing every one to two years.

Ride-on mowers These are invaluable for very big gardens. They move faster than you could walk and have an extra-wide cutting width that makes quick work of even the largest lawns. They are not, however, suitable for fine lawns.

Reciprocating knife mowers Best suited to long grass and light scrub, these have been almost superseded by the trimmer. They have two toothed bars set one above the other. As the upper 'cutter' bar moves out and back across the lower one, the grass is trapped between the blades and cut. This type of mower is usually engine-driven and self-propelled.

shorter grass for a neater finish or longer for greater drought-tolerance, by raising and lowering the wheels, moving the rotating disc assembly up and down, or using spacers between the motor and the rotating disc.

Keep the blades sharp and free of dried grass in order to cut properly and replace them if they are damaged by hitting a stone or other obstruction. After use, clean any grass off the blade(s) and wipe clean with an oily cloth. With average use, the blades will need sharpening or replacing every two years.

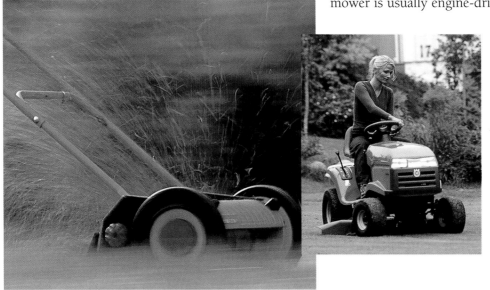

The two extremes

The simplest mower is the reel mower (far left), which is best suited to small lawns; ride-on mowers are expensive, but take the hard work out of cutting a large expanse of lawn.

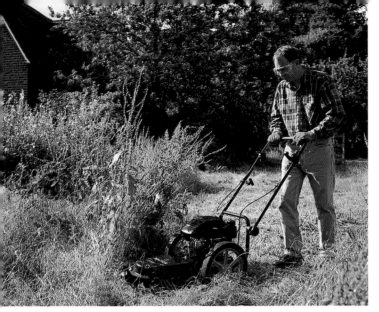

Reciprocating knife mower

If you have large, overgrown areas in your garden, this machine will efficiently tackle heavy undergrowth or scrubby grass.

The power source can be either petrol, mains electricity or battery. They typically have a cutting diameter of about 25 cm, cable length of 12 metres, an alloy shaft and a polypropylene hand grip. The hand grip may rotate to make working at an angle easier, and the nylon cord may be manual- or tap-fed.

If your trimmer has an electric lead, always keep it over one shoulder so you can't cut through it, and use a residual current device (see page 128).

Flail mowers These are useful for coarse grass or areas of light scrub, and can deal with grass up to a metre high, although they are losing ground today to the trimmer. The mower incorporates a horizontal rotor carrying a number of swinging metal flails turning at high speed. Each flail has a cutting edge and is held in its cutting position by centrifugal force.

Nylon-cord trimmers These are really rotary scythes, with nylon cord feeding out from a spool and rotating at high speed. They are ideal for trimming weeds and grass in inaccessible areas. Their great attraction is that the nylon cord does not damage brickwork, so you can trim right up to the base of a wall or the edge of a path, where the mower will not cut. They will also cut around trees and gateposts – in fact, almost anything which usually gets in the way of a mower.

Keep your garden trim

For awkward, hard-to-reach spots such as around trees, under over-hanging plants and hedges, and next to walls and fences, a trimmer should be your choice of tool. The nylon cord (inset) revolves at high speed, cutting as it turns. As the cord wears away, more can be fed out to replace it.

> **'Nothing is more pleasant to the eye than green grass kept finely shorn.'**
>
> FRANCIS BACON, PHILOSOPHER AND ESSAYIST (1561–1626)

HAND TOOLS

These add the finishing touch once the mechanized tools have done the bulk of the work. Their smaller size allows you to work in confined spaces and tidy up anything the larger tools have left behind. As you work, you can also check the health of the plants and the lawn to see if any remedial action needs to be taken.

SHEARS

The manual alternative to the powered trimmer in inaccessible areas is a pair of lawn shears. They closely resemble their hedging counterparts, but with the addition of long handles so you can work standing upright with blades set at an angle. Comfort grips and shock absorbers on the handles make them easy to use, and the blades often have a non-stick coating to help them cut more easily and resist sap. If you have only a small area of rough grass to cut – or just want

For awkward corners of lawn

Tidy up areas around trees and other obstacles that aren't tackled by your mower using a pair of long-handled lawn shears.

the anatomy of **shears**

Look for smooth handles of wood (ash is a popular choice) or polypropylene for a lighter-weight option. Specialist lawn shears are available with long handles, which enable you to work from a standing position. Some models have ergonomically designed handles: try them out to make sure they suit you.

Stainless steel or carbon steel are the best materials for the blades. Shock absorbers (usually in the form of rubber stoppers) at the base of the blades will take the strain from your wrists.

to trim long grass straggling from the lawn into the border – these are an economic alternative to the mechanical variety. Some models have telescopic handles so they can be adjusted to the most comfortable working length.

Small, single-handed shears are sometimes sold as grass shears and will cut in even the most restricted areas. They have scissor-like blades which swivel through 180 degrees so you can use them horizontally, vertically or at an angle, and left- or right-handed.

EDGING TOOLS

There are two main edging tools: edging shears and edging irons. The former are used to emphasize the boundary of a lawn. They have scissor-like blades set at 90 degrees to the long handles, so that you can work upright and sideways along the edge of the lawn to the left or right. Use them to finish off the lawn after mowing, neaten all the edges, and you can even buy shears that catch the cuttings. A battery-powered version with two rows of toughened, steel blades can be used kneeling or standing (with a telescopic extension handle).

Finishing touches

Grass shears (far left) are useful for small patches of grass and for cutting areas out of the reach of the mower. Border shears (left) make easy work of tidying the edge of the lawn, once you have finished mowing.

The edging iron (or half-moon) is an alternative to shears, with a sharp, semi-circular blade mounted on a spade handle. Use it to re-cut an uneven or crumbling lawn edge by driving it down vertically with the foot to separate the unwanted edge. You may only need it three or four times during the growing season, whereas the edging shears may be used every 14 days when the grass is growing vigorously.

GRUBBERS

These are small, hand-held tools for removing individual daisies and other weeds from the lawn causing as little disturbance as possible to the surrounding grass, or for weeding in difficult places like the cracks between paving. The so-called 'weed grubber' has a short, narrow blade with a V-cut end on a metal shaft, and the 'daisy grubber' has two short prongs on a long, narrow blade.

Both are mounted into the (usually) wooden handle with a tang-and-ferrule and are used by driving them down into the ground immediately next to the

Weeding your lawn

To root out individual weeds such as daisies and dandelions, use a daisy grubber. The forked blade enables you to work underneath deep taproots, so that you can be sure of removing the whole plant.

offending weed. Use leverage gently to bring out the roots of the plant without taking too much soil or surrounding grass as well. The blade of the daisy grubber may be angled for easier use.

AERATORS

If your lawn has become compacted by waterlogging or being walked on, you need to loosen the soil again, and the easiest way to do this is to use an aerator. These range from a simple pair of overshoes with spikes on the underside which you use to walk over

If your lawn is a large one, an electric aerator will come in handy. As you push it across the grass, the spikes at the bottom penetrate the ground, enabling air, water and nutrients to reach the roots more easily.

not remove thatch regularly, it builds up to the extent that the grass starts to root into the thatch rather than the soil beneath, making your lawn weak and susceptible to drought and fungal attack. Scarifying your lawn every month or two encourages the growth of stronger, healthier grass.

If you have a large expanse of lawn, use a mechanical scarifier with a spiked drum that combs the thatch out. Ideally the scarifying tines should be set so that they penetrate to the soil's surface. For the smaller plot, however, a hand-operated version is perfectly adequate. This consists of a metal head with about 24 tines on a straight bar, attached to a long, wooden handle. It resembles a flexible rake but has stronger tines.

FLEXIBLE RAKES

The fan rake (sometimes known as a 'springbok') can also be used for removing dead material (thatch) from the lawn, as well as any moss or dead leaves in autumn. It has fine, circular, wire-like, metal tines in a fan shape, curved towards their ends and held in place

the lawn, to large machines with hollow, solid or flat tines mounted on a drum which is pushed or propelled over the lawn. Although solid tines open up vertical channels in the lawn through which air can enter, the area between holes is compacted even more to create them. By removing plugs of soil (which can be used as top-dressing when they have dried), you can fill the holes with quick-draining sharp sand. This will speed up drainage and open up the soil generally, as the organisms within the soil mix the sand in.

The manual aerator has a spade-like handle of wood or metal (or two straight handles with a cross piece at the top), and two to four tines on a horizontal bar that you push vertically into the ground with your foot and pull up again. The tines should be about 15 cm long to be fully effective and penetrate the compacted layer of soil about 10 cm below the surface.

SCARIFIERS

The term 'scarifying' is given to the removal of dead material known as thatch from a lawn where it accumulates at the base of the grass plants. If you do

When the roots are properly nourished, the grass will look thicker and greener. Scarifiers range from compact manual models, which are suitable for small lawns, to large heavy-duty electric or petrol-driven machines.

Keep your lawn tidy

Fallen leaves not only spoil the appearance of a pristine lawn, but also can encourage diseases and yellowing if they are left to decompose. A springy lawn rake (such as the plastic version, left) will allow you to quickly skim leaves and other debris from the surface of the grass before they can do any damage.

ROLLERS

These are intended to flatten any bumps in the lawn and encourage tillering, but are heavy and seldom needed on the average lawn, as their weight can cause soil compaction. The roller of a cylinder mower is just as good for its tillering effect, whilst imperfections can be cured by lifting and re-laying horizontally a small area of turf.

against a sturdy metal frame. Adjust the tines to increase or reduce the width of the fan, depending on the space available. The rake will comb through the grass, snagging any debris, including autumn leaves and grass clippings, and pulling it out as it goes. Bamboo and plastic versions are also available. See pages 31 and 98–9 for further information on rakes.

TURFING IRONS

Used for lifting turf which is to be relaid, the turfing iron is designed to slide underneath the grass, lifting the grass and the soil in which its roots grow. It has a flat, heart-shaped, carbon-steel head on an angled shaft, which in turn attaches to a wooden, spade-type handle. Choose a point about 2 or 3 cm below the soil surface and use short pushing strokes to slide the iron horizontally beneath the turf.

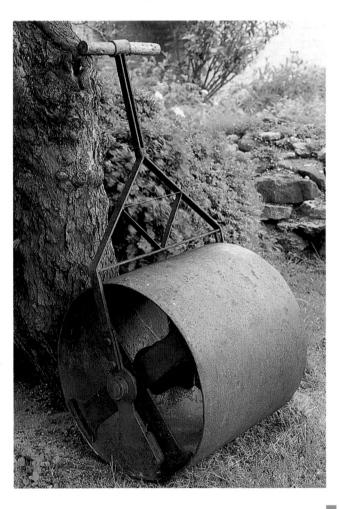

Smooth out the bumps

Lumps and bumps can turn into unsightly bare patches after mowing, which is why some gardeners like to use a roller. Traditionally, lawn rollers were very heavy iron implements. Today, most models consist of a hollow reinforced plastic drum, which you fill with water to add weight.

Pruning and cutting tools

In the garden, you will regularly find you need to trim something or other. It may be as small as a stray shoot or spent flower, but now and again, it will be larger, such as removing an overhanging branch for safety reasons. Always bear in mind that the right tool for the job makes the task in hand much easier.

The equipment needed for this task varies considerably from the small and lightweight through to large, heavy-duty, professional tools. Every gardener needs a good pair of secateurs, as they are so versatile, but not everyone needs something as large as a chain saw. Tools like this, unless you have a very large plot, are best hired as and when you need them.

The other tools in this category will find their way into your collection as your interest in gardening develops. Venturing into fruit-growing, for instance, may well mean investing in long-handled pruners. Taking up propagating your own plants will mean getting at least one good knife, and planting a hedge will necessitate buying shears or a hedge trimmer. Hiring is a good means of trying out different tools before you buy, to see if you really do need your own, and if so, which are the right ones for you.

Your choice of cutting tools will be governed by the plants you are growing, although a good pair of secateurs are an asset to any gardener. If your heavy pruning is a once-a-year blitz, then it is worth considering hiring the equipment, rather than housing it unused for the other eleven months. If you buy your own, look for a good brand, as cheaper tools are more liable to break as you use them, causing damage to the plant, you, or both.

Cutting tools are designed to cut – an obvious statement, but it means that they cannot do the task they were intended for if they are not sharp. They should be stored in a dry, frost-free place, cleaned thoroughly after each use, wiped regularly with an oily cloth to prevent rust and taken for professional sharpening every one to three years, depending on how often they are used. See Chapter 9 for more information on maintaining your cutting tools.

Bypass secateurs
The curved blades hold the stem in place and make a clean cut, helping to protect the plant from pests and disease.

SECATEURS

You can't beat a good pair of sharp secateurs for most types of pruning. They are as essential to the gardener as the plants themselves and, once you find a pair to suit your hands, you will use them for years. They are intended for light pruning of woody plants, but most can cut through shoots up to finger thickness: you will need loppers to cut anything bigger than this. Secateurs are also useful for deadheading, cutting flowers for indoors and preparing cuttings for

Anvil secateurs

The sharp upper blade cuts down onto a softer flat anvil, slicing through the branch or stem. The cut is slightly stronger than that of bypass secateurs, making them ideal for hard, woody growth.

problem – even in a tight corner if necessary; and check that you can easily operate the safety lock, which keeps the blades closed when not in use.

CHOOSING THE RIGHT SECATEURS

Most are made of carbon steel, and the blade(s) may be coated with a non-stick material to make cutting easier and reduce the chance of sap fouling them. The

the anatomy of **secateurs**

Handles should be moulded with a non-slip grip, allowing you to easily manoeuvre amongst the branches of your plants.

The safety lock should be well positioned for maximum ease of use, and should be simply operated with the flick of your thumb.

Blades should be replaceable and may be coated with a non-stick finish to prevent rust and reduce friction.Some models have a sap groove in the blade.

propagation. They should not be used for cutting wire (which will damage the blade) or ripping into bags of compost (which may get into the mechanism).

Really good secateurs will have an expensive price tag, but they are a worthwhile investment. If you spend as much as you can afford, they will repay you by lasting a lifetime, with just a little regular care. Do try them out before you buy, because different brands suit different hand sizes, and some springs are stiffer than others. Most manufacturers make both right- and left-handed secateurs, as well as some with an ambidextrous grip and thumb catch. Look for a brand with replaceable blades, too.

When trying them out, test the weight in your hand; try extending the handles (are they too wide for you?); ensure you can open and close the blades with no hand grips are generally fibreglass, moulded nylon or lightweight aluminium alloy coated in moulded vinyl to ensure they don't slip while cutting. Look for a shock absorber between the handles which will save injuring your fingers.

You will find several different types of secateurs in your local garden centre:

Bypass (or parrot-bill) secateurs have two curved blades which bypass one another very closely and cut in a scissor-like action. This is the most popular type of secateur and is ideal for your more delicate plants, as the cut is very precise.

Anvil secateurs chop like a knife, with a single straight-edged cutting blade that closes down onto a flat bar of metal (often brass) called an anvil. These are not quite as easy to manoeuvre between tight branches as their bypass cousins, and can also slightly crush the stems as they cut. However, they are better at tackling hard woody stems.

Blade and half-anvil secateurs have one convex cutting blade which cuts past a second, fixed curved bar, in a bypass cutting action.

Manaresi secateurs have two blades, both with straight cutting edges, which meet as the cutting action is completed. These are often preferred for pruning vines.

Ratchet-action anvil secateurs have a special mechanism (the ratchet) that enables you to cut through a branch in stages. Each time you squeeze the handle, the blade works deeper into the stem, until it is cut right through. These are good for reducing fatigue and are ideal for gardeners with a smaller hand span, although the cutting action is slower than that of conventional models.

HOW TO USE SECATEURS

Always position the stem to be cut close to the base of the blade where it can be held firmly. If the cut is made with the tip, the blades are liable to be strained or forced apart. Always make a clean, straight cut – don't twist the secateurs or your wrist. If you can't cut through cleanly, the stem may be too thick and you may need to use loppers instead.

Each type of secateur can produce a good, clean cut if used correctly and provided it is kept clean, sharp and in good condition.

Pruning a shrub or ground-cover rose

1 If you are pruning a rose or other thorny shrub, be sure to wear thick gloves. First use the secateurs to cut back the long shoots. This will allow you to start shaping the bush.

2 Cut out any old or diseased wood as close to the main stem as possible.

3 The finished shrub should remain in a good shape with strong, healthy stems bearing flowering shoots.

After use, wipe the blade(s) to get rid of any sap that has accumulated, and allow them to dry before closing them up. Wipe them regularly with an oily cloth and keep the pivoting bolt oiled so that it moves freely and does not strain the wrist. If the secateurs have a spring, oil it in spring and autumn to repel rust and keep it moving easily.

The blade(s) will need sharpening with an oil stone at least once a season, and more often if they are used intensively. In the event of serious damage, many manufacturers sell replacement blades, and some even have a servicing department that can overhaul your secateurs if necessary.

LOPPERS

These tools resemble long-handled secateurs and have a similar bypass or anvil blade arrangement. Loppers are used to cut through woody stems which would be too thick for traditional secateurs, and are ideal for removing old stems on vigorous shrubs like philadelphus or for cutting out old rose stumps that can build up at the base of bushes. The long handles give you good leverage on thicker stems and will reach into or up to branches you could not otherwise cut. Make sure there are shock-absorbing stoppers.

LONG-ARM PRUNERS

These pole pruners are used for pruning tree branches which would normally be out of reach, and can cut through branches up to 2 or 3 cm thick. They consist of a pole 2–3 metres in length with a hooked anvil and curved blade at the tip, the blade operated by a lever at the opposite end.

Some models are available with an interchangeable pruning saw or a small basket attachment which fits close to the blade for picking fruit without the need to use a ladder. However, doing this from below means you must take care not to remove next year's fruit buds at harvest time.

SMALL CUTTING TOOLS

Floral scissors are used for the very lightest of cutting around the garden, shaping house plants and for flower arranging. They have large handgrips in relation to the size of the blades, and thin, finely pointed blades for accuracy. For more information on cutting fresh flowers, turn to pages 88–9.

Powerful cutting

The long handles on loppers give you greater leverage then secateurs, meaning you can cut larger branches.

Garden snips look like a cross between scissors and bypass secateurs, but they have much narrower blades than secateurs and are used for tasks such as thinning and harvesting grapes.

KNIVES

Gardening knives come in dozens of shapes and sizes, each suited to a different purpose. Whichever model you choose should be well-balanced, strong, light and comfortable to use, with a sharp cutting edge.

General-purpose knives are ideal for the rough jobs in the garden, such as cutting string and opening bags of compost or fertilizer. They may have just one blade, or a multitude of accessories in the one unit.

Care should always be taken when handling a knife, particularly when closing it, so that it does not snap shut on your fingers. Clean the blade thoroughly after use to get rid of any sap. Wipe it with an oily rag occasionally to keep it rust-free (removing any remaining oil before using it again). A knife in regular use will need sharpening every few weeks, and it is worth getting a fine sharpening stone to keep the

THE MAKING OF KNIVES

Like good-quality cutlery, a garden knife should be comfortable to hold and feel satisfyingly heavy in your hand. It should have a razor-sharp blade that makes the cleanest of cuts and, if it's of the folding variety, should open and close easily, even with wet hands. The best folding knives have a locking mechanism to prevent the blade from closing while you are using it.

Many factory-made knives are first-rate, but the crème de la crème are the hand-crafted models. These can be expensive, but they will last you a lifetime. Particularly interesting are knives that marry traditional manufacturing techniques with a modern design or materials.

Handmade pocket knives

The basic shapes for the handle and blade are laser cut from sheets of steel, and then shaped, sharpened, and polished by hand.

1 FOLDING THE HANDLE Made from one piece of metal, the handle is folded in half to create a receptacle for the blade.

2 TIGHTENING THE HANDLE Once folded, the metal is placed in a vice to achieve a neat space into which the blade can fit.

3 CREATING THE BLADES The flat pieces of metal for the blades are ground down to a fine point.

4 ASSEMBLING THE COMPONENTS After the metal has been heat treated and then quenched by liquid nitrogen to harden the steel, the blades and handles are fixed together, and the finishing process and polishing begins.

A clean cut

You will need a cutting knife with a straight blade (left) for working on your potting bench. This knife (centre) allows you to remove a stem with minimal damage to the parent plant. A curved blade (right) is helpful for slicing into rootstocks.

blade in the best condition. Too coarse a stone will wear the blade away very quickly. (See pages 148–9 for advice on sharpening knives.)

Pruning knives You can identify a pruning knife by its weight, its bulky, often curved handle and its concave blade. The curve of the blade helps when cutting through thicker shoots. Some also have a mini-saw which folds into the handle.

Budding knives Blunt-ended, these are used when propagating plants, such as roses, by transferring the bud from a selected variety to a rootstock. They are light and thin-bladed because of the delicate nature of the work they do, slicing thin segments of plant tissue without causing excessive damage. They also tend to have a curved knob or 'bark lifter' at the end of the blade which, if you twist the knife after making a cut in the stock, will hold open the cut while you insert the bud with the other hand.

Grafting and cuttings knives Both grafting and cuttings knives have similar straight blades, but the handle of the grafting knife is usually curved, whereas that of the cuttings knife is slimmer and straight. The grafting knife is used for propagating plants, such as conifers, by transferring a piece of the selected variety to a rootstock. The cuttings knife is used for taking all types of cuttings (short pieces of shoot which can form roots and grow) from selected plants.

HEDGE TOOLS

Once your hedge has reached its optimum height, you will have to trim it to keep it vigorous and healthy. Whether you choose a hand-operated, electric or fuel-powered hedge trimmer will usually be governed by how much hedge you have to cut and how often it needs doing. For a short or slow-growing hedge such as yew or box which needs cutting only a few times each season, hand shears will probably suffice whereas for a long or fast-growing coniferous hedge you may need the help of a powered tool to speed things up.

Cutting your hedge regularly will keep the growth young and bushy, ensuring that the hedge looks attractive and the shoots you are trimming are not too tough and woody for the equipment. Always cut from the base of the hedge upwards, so that the cut material can fall freely to the ground, rather than interfering with the work.

SHEARS

Hand-operated hedge shears come in several designs, but they should be strong, light and comfortable to use, with a sharp cutting edge. Most have straight, carbon steel blades with a deep notch at the base of the blade for cutting thicker stems. Some may even have a non-stick coating for easier cutting and cleaning.

When buying hedge shears, look for comfortable grips, moulded to suit your hands; a blade length to suit your use (from 15 to 20 cm); an adjustable tension nut; and shock absorbers to prevent jarring and injury to your wrists.

To reach across a wide hedge, it is possible to get telescopic shears with handles that extend from 30 to 50 cm and lock into position. The handles may be made of wood, polypropylene or aluminium, and the weight will vary accordingly. Choose the pair that suits you, and remember, you may be using them for some time if you have to do a lot of cutting, and the weight will increase as your arms get tired.

Single-handed shears Although they will only deal with small, soft shoots, single-handed hedge shears are useful for giving the hedge a tidy-up between its regular cuttings. They are sold by some manufacturers as grass-cutting shears, and have a squeeze grip and two scissor-like blades. The blades swivel around 90 degrees so you can cut a horizontal or vertical plane.

HEDGE TRIMMERS

These are a quick mechanical means of cutting a hedge, and are ideal for gardeners with large expanses of vigorous hedging. Hedge trimmers have two blades,

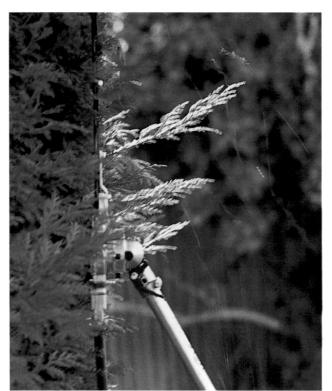

one on top of the other, each with teeth so that as one blade is drawn backwards and forwards, the shoots are trapped between the teeth and cut. They may be powered by mains electricity, battery or petrol. The weight will vary according to the power source and the length of the cutting blade, so select one you can use at any angle on the hedge and with which you will feel comfortable for a prolonged period.

If your hedge is near the power point, choose an electric model that is light, easy and convenient. However, dragging the cable behind you over a long distance is more difficult and should not be undertaken in wet conditions. It is also essential to keep the cable well away from the working area so there is no danger of cutting through it.

Battery-powered cordless trimmers are light, easy to use and have a detachable, rechargeable power supply. How long this will last as you cut depends on what you are cutting. More power is needed to cut older, thicker branches and dense wood such as yew, beech and hornbeam. Thinner, regularly-pruned wood, such as forsythia and privet, is easier to cut through, and the power reserve will last longer.

Petrol-driven hedge trimmers have a motor in the handle and are consequently heavier to operate. The

Pruning hedging conifers

Large vertical plants such as leylandii can be difficult to trim: the head of this petrol-powered trimmer swivels so that you can use it at any angle.

Cut down to size

A garden saw (opposite page) is a sturdy implement for pruning most trees. Thick branches and logs are best tackled with a bow saw (far left). Many pruning saws (left) fold away into the handle after use for safe transit and storage.

blade may be inter-changeable with a trimmer attachment for cutting rough grass and brambles. This type of trimmer is suitable if you are operating at a great distance from a power source and cutting tough, woody hedges. Rather than purchase a heavy-duty piece of equipment like this, it may be better to hire it for the few times you will need it during the season.

SAWS AND LARGE CUTTING TOOLS

Saws have a multitude of uses in the larger garden, especially if you have trees. The larger ones can be used for cutting up whole trees or branches which blow down in the wind, removing diseased limbs or those growing outside their allotted space. The smaller saws can be used on woody shrubs and small trees to thin congested growth and remove damaged shoots. Choose the right type of blade for the job in hand: a short blade with closely spaced teeth is best for dealing with smaller branches; use a long-bladed saw with less densely spaced teeth for really thick branches.

When buying a new saw, look for a narrow, rounded nose which allows you to work in a tight corner without damaging other branches, and tough, tempered steel blades. Try the grip and make sure it is comfortable, with a knuckle protector in case your hand slips. If you choose a folding saw, make sure it has a lock that you can secure in both open and closed positions.

When using a saw, hold the branch beyond the cutting point with your free hand so that it doesn't tear off as the cut deepens, which would damage the trunk. Pause periodically while you are cutting to clear the teeth of sawdust which will inhibit the cutting action. Clean the blade thoroughly after use and wipe occasionally with an oily cloth.

Bow saws These have a curved steel tubing frame and a straight cutting blade with a row of sharp teeth on the outside. The blade is held taut between the arms of the frame and is released by a handle at one end. Use a bow saw for working through larger branches and logs; it will cut on both the forward and return strokes. They vary in size, shape and blade length, but the blades are replaceable and for cutting larger branches, they are ideal. Keep a cover over the blade when it is not in use.

Garden saws The general-purpose garden saw is much like a wood saw in that it is a basic triangular shape with teeth along one edge. It is useful for pruning trees and shrubs and cutting logs and larger branches where access is difficult for a bow saw. It has small teeth at the tip of the blade to help start off, then larger teeth along the blade for faster cutting. It cuts on both the forward and backward stroke.

Pruning saws Small, hand-held tools with a straight or curved steel blade, pruning saws are useful for cutting larger branches. Several models are available which are particularly suitable for use in small spaces and in the narrow angles between branches.

Many are designed to fold, with the blade closing into the handle like a knife for easy storage. These fit neatly into a pocket when not in use, so can be carried around as you go without being a nuisance, but are better used on only moderately thick branches.

Topiary tool kit

The art of shaping and training trees and shrubs has been popular with gardeners for centuries. A lively imagination and a certain amount of patience are the most important tools you'll need, along with some sharp cutting implements.

One of the great things about topiary is that it looks just as at home in a small courtyard or patio as it does in a large, formal garden. A pair of globe-shaped bay trees in containers provide an eye-catching frame for a doorway; a living sculpture makes an arresting impression in front of your home; low box hedges are a good way of creating boundaries for a herb garden; while a small, ivy-covered wire frame can make a great centrepiece for your dinner table.

Many plants are suitable for topiary. Evergreens are favourites as they provide year-round interest in the garden. For large geometric shapes, bay (*Laurus nobilis*) and holly (*Ilex aquifolium*) are good choices. Box (*Buxus sempervirens*) and slow-growing yew (*Taxus baccata*) are ideal for more complex shapes. Sphagnum moss is good for stuffing wire frames. And creeping fig (*Ficus pumila*) and ivy (*Hedera helix*) are easy to train round wire supports.

Trimming implements

Sharp cutting tools are essential if you are to achieve a tidy finish. Large-scale topiary may require electric hedge trimmers to get you started and enable you to establish the basic shape, but trimmers are too crude for the finishing touches.

Good-quality hedge shears are perfect for trimming box hedges in knot gardens and creating straightforward geometric shapes. Scissors or secateurs are better for complicated shapes such as animals

Shape up your plants

Growing trailing plants over a wire frame is a quick and easy way of creating a topiary effect (far left and centre left). Topiary shears (left) offer maximum control when precision cutting is necessary.

Creating a shape

Cones, spirals and spheres; rabbits, ducks, and other animals; waves, hearts and abstract designs – you can grow or trim a plant into any shape that inspires you. There are three ways to achieve your aims: you can trim a shrub to the desired shape, which, depending on the design, can be quite a skilled technique; you can train plants to grow over a wire frame; or you can stuff a frame with moss.

If you are trimming a hedge or shrub into a solid shape, you will probably find it easier to use guides. String and bamboo canes are helpful when you are trying to create a straight line. For curves and more complicated lines, you can use stiff wire.

Frames are available in many different designs from garden centres and websites. These may be two-dimensional shapes, such as hearts and stars, or three-dimensional ones like cones, spirals and animals. The two-dimensional versions are mainly designed for climbing plants like ivy or creeping fig; simply insert the frame into the ground or container and trail the stems of your plant around the wire as it grows.

For a more solid living sculpture, you'll need to place a three-dimensional frame over a plant growing in the ground or in a container. As the plant grows, its leaves will start to fill the frame and eventually protrude through the wire – simply trim them back to the shape of the frame.

It isn't difficult to make a simple frame yourself, however: all you need is some sturdy wire and a pair of wire cutters (don't use secateurs, as the wire will blunt the blades).

Quick topiary

Box, yew, bay and other traditional topiary plants are quite slow-growing, so you don't have to spend all your precious gardening time trimming and pruning. The downside is that it can take several years to create a topiary shape. For more instant results, you can stuff a wire frame with sphagnum moss and then plant it up, a bit like a hanging basket, with fast-growing vining plants. Eventually these plants will spread over the frame, completely hiding the moss. You'll need chicken wire or plastic mesh to cover the frame, clear fishing line to hold the moss in place and a good pair of gloves, as sphagnum moss can contain bacteria that may cause infection if it comes into contact with an abrasion. Old hairpins are useful for holding the new growth in place.

Keep it neat

Cutting in a straight line can be tricky, especially when you are working at an awkward height, so use a length of garden string to help you avoid mistakes.

and spirals. Specialized topiary shears will be very useful if you are a real enthusiast. Held in one hand, these consist of two razor-sharp, carbon-steel blades that are worked by squeezing the double bow shaped handles together. The grip position gives you precise control over the cut and you can catch the cuttings with your free hand.

English pruning saws These have a tapering blade with teeth on both sides, one set producing a smoother finished cut than the other. Take care while sawing not to damage nearby branches with the set of teeth not in use.

The Grecian saw This has a curved blade tapered to a sharp point and sloping teeth designed to cut on the return stroke. The teeth are large and coarse to enable them to cut through soft, wet, live wood.

Straight-bladed saws The shape of the teeth varies according to whether it is designed to cut on just the return (pull) stroke or on both the push and return.

CHAIN SAWS

These are heavy-duty cutting tools, used for felling trees and cutting up larger logs. They may be powered by electricity or petrol and operate as the motor sends a toothed, cutting chain travelling around the perimeter of a long, oval, metal guide bar. The petrol-driven types are heavier than electric ones and they come in a range of sizes according to their intended use. Choose one which feels balanced in your hands and has a good guard over the grip to protect your hand. Unless you have a lot of woodland, you are unlikely to need a chain saw very often, and it will

Cutting and clearing tools
A well-stocked shed would include a scythe, a rake and a hay fork (the long-handled tools at the front); a sickle leans in the lower right corner of the doorway.

probably be as easy to hire one for a day. Safety is paramount when operating a chain saw (see page 129) as it is sharp, fast-moving and heavy. Plus, if there is a knot in the wood you are cutting, the bar will kick back out. You will need gloves, goggles, ear protection, steel-toed boots and a helmet as basic essentials. Snag-proof trousers are a bonus too. Long hair must be tied out of the way, and you should take off, or fasten, any loose clothing.

THE SCYTHE

This is a very sharp, curved, carbon-steel blade mounted on a long, wood or tubular steel shaft (the snath), with a wooden handgrip at the top and

Go for the chop
Use an axe (far left) to chop larger logs, and a hatchet (left) to cut up kindling and small branches.

another adjustable one mounted part way down to make it easier to use. It is useful for cutting through long or rough grass, and the heavier models can also cut through bramble stems and scrub. It was the traditional implement used for harvesting corn, and an accomplished user can quickly cut through a large area with a rhythmic swinging motion – and a very sharp blade. The length of the swing needed to wield this properly means that it is not easy to stop if you spot an obstruction, so it is best used on areas you know to be without large stones. Clean, sharpen and wipe the blade over with an oily cloth after each use to keep the effort needed to use it to a minimum.

SICKLE
This consists of a very sharp curved blade mounted on a short wooden or plastic handle. You should use it low down to the ground for trimming rough grass where rocks may be hidden. It needs to be kept very sharp to work well and most are made for right-handed users, so may be difficult for left-handed gardeners to wield.

BILLHOOKS
Traditionally used for hedgerow maintenance and hedge laying, the billhook has a sharp, curved blade – like a bird's beak – often with a flat-edged blade on the back. It can be mounted on a short handle for closer work (with rivets or a tang-and-ferrule joint), or on a longer hickory shaft (with rivets) for tasks like hacking through tough undergrowth.

Similar implements are available, known as slashers or brush hooks. These also have a long shaft and a curved blade for cutting through brush and thickets. Reap and grass hooks are hand-held, with a long, curved blade for cutting through rough grass and overgrown weeds.

AXES AND HATCHETS
The axe is not a subtle implement, but it is unrivalled for splitting logs and chopping out old tree stumps. It consists of a delta-shaped, carbon-steel head, tempered and hardened for durability, and fitted onto a wooden handle. The wood used is often hickory, chosen for its strength, and should be smooth and splinter-free. The head should also be smooth-looking, with no obvious blemishes where it could crack under strain. Use all sizes of axe in a swinging motion, employing two hands. The hatchet is essentially a smaller version of the axe, with a shorter handle that you can use with one hand.

SHREDDERS
Garden shredders are designed to make light work of chopping prunings, fallen leaves and other debris into a manageable mulch. It is important to consider the size of your garden and how much waste it will generate before you buy a shredder. If you only shred once or twice a year, you may as well hire one for the day rather than have it sitting in the shed. However, if you make your own compost and are likely to shred everything you prune throughout the year, it will be a good investment. See page 101 for more on shredders.

5

Planting
and Sowing

The potting bench

Planting and sowing are two of the most exciting aspects of gardening because they represent new beginnings and the promise of things to come. It's hard to beat the thrilling sense of achievement you feel when the first tiny shoots start to appear on the first plants you grow from seed. As they get larger, your next target is to keep them healthy as you move them outside or into larger pots. Plants that you buy when young and vulnerable require similar care and provide similar exciting rewards.

PLANTING TOOLS

The tools for the first stage in a plant's life are necessarily small, to deal with the detailed handling involved. Using too large an implement could mean a clumsy loss of control proving fatal to a delicate little plant. You should also prepare the soil to a fine tilth for the seedlings to survive – even if you are sowing seed directly into a seedbed outdoors (as with vegetables, for instance). If you try to sow seed where the soil lumps are large there will be too many air pockets, and a tiny root will wither before it reaches its target of soil. Marking out the rows before you start will allow you to track where you have sown the seed, and clear markers will remind you what it was.

MEASURING RODS

If you are marking out several rows for seeds or planting a hedge with the plants at set spacings, then one of the easiest ways of keeping the distance consistent is to use a measuring rod. This is a piece of wood, about 2 metres long, marked at 7–15 cm intervals. Lay it on the ground next to where you are working, and use the marks to determine your

Growing your own

If you have the space, dedicate an area of your garden shed to potting (right). Here you can store unused containers and work comfortably at a potting bench. Young plants are difficult to tell apart, so make sure you label them (above).

Soil scoop

This tool has a sharp point that enables you to dig small holes, and serrated edges to cut through root bound soil. The curved tip prevents soil from slipping off.

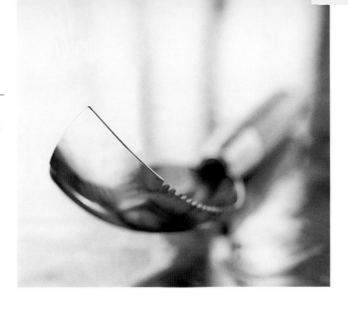

spacings. For close spacings, use every mark, but for wider gaps, use alternate marks or one in three. You can make your own measuring rod by calibrating a long piece of wood or straight bamboo cane.

GARDEN LINE

To allow you to work along a straight line between two points you will need a garden line. This strong twine or polypropylene thread is brightly coloured – usually orange – making it easy to spot and avoid when it is lying against the soil. Wind it around two metal or plastic spools, each with a spike to drive it firmly into the soil. Make a loop with the twine to fit over the spike before pushing it into the ground to stop surplus twine passing out and distorting the line you are trying to keep.

A garden line is useful for marking out a drill for sowing seed in the vegetable garden, although you can just as easily use it to mark the edge of a lawn you are laying or re-cutting. Sow the seed in the drill, cover it lightly with soil and simply lift the line to move to the next position.

LABELS

With all the work involved in planting or sowing, it is easy to overlook the task of labelling the plants – the most obvious method of recording what has been sown or planted and when. If they are beyond the seedling stage, with obvious markings, flower colours, or leaf shapes, then you should find it easy to distinguish one from another. Where you are sowing seed, however, this is much more difficult, as seedlings often have very similar seed leaves, especially within the same plant family (as with vegetables).

When you have regular crops, you can use plastic labels season after season. Clean them between crops if you change variety, or write them in permanent marker for use with the same one. Where you are planting more permanently with shrubs, climbers and trees in the garden, you can use an ornamental label – such as metal or plastic tape – with the letters embossed on it.

TROWEL

Hand trowels have a multitude of uses within the garden, their size making them suitable for many detailed tasks (see page 36). The width of the trowel head varies slightly according to whether it is designed for general garden tasks, or a narrower transplanting trowel more suited to thinning out and replanting seedlings and small plants. Use it like a small spade: for pushing under the plant and lifting it out of the soil, or for digging a small planting hole.

Planting out

A measuring rod (left) is invaluable when planting at even distances is important. Use a garden line (centre) to sow in a straight line. Labels come in a huge range of shapes and sizes (right).

If the blade of the trowel has depth markings on it, it is intended primarily for planting bulbs. The markings are a quick and easy guide to how deep you are pushing the trowel into the soil, as you plant each bulb at its appropriate depth. Too deep and the bulb may not live long enough for the shoot to reach the surface. Too shallow and it may push itself out of the soil as the roots develop, or you may damage it as you

Specialist trowels

A calibrated trowel (far left) is especially helpful when the depth of planting is critical, for example when transplanting or planting bulbs. A right-angled trowel (left) is perfect for transferring seedlings into the ground: simply pull the blade towards you to open a hole in the soil and then pop in the plant.

Bulb planters

These can be short-handled (below) or long-handled (right). The latter often have a T-bar at the base to press down on with your foot.

cultivate nearby soil. A bulb-planting trowel is also useful for transplanting, where you need to set all young plants at the same depth.

You can find trowels made entirely of polypropylene, or with heads of carbon steel, stainless steel or aluminium with a tang-and-ferrule joint into a wooden handle. Carbon-steel models may have a non-stick coating to reduce the chance of corrosion or soil sticking to them (making them heavier to use). Some have ergonomic handles to ease strain on the wrists.

HAND FORK

Like the hand trowel, the diminutive size of the hand fork means that it is suited to close, detailed work. Use one hand fork to prepare a small area of soil for planting – such as a seedbed between established plants – or use two forks back-to-back to divide an established plant. You can split a congested clump of iris into several smaller clumps and replant them further apart by pushing both forks into the large clump, together but back-to-back, and then prise them apart to divide the matted growth. Repeat this until the new clumps are the required size and give any surplus away to friends – trading for new varieties – or compost them.

Forks may be made of polypropylene throughout, or with a head of carbon steel, stainless steel or aluminium with a wooden handle. As with trowels, carbon-steel models often have a non-stick coating.

BULB PLANTERS

The easiest way to plant a number of bulbs for a massed effect is to consign them to a trench or hole. However, if you are planting bulbs individually, then a bulb planter is a useful tool. It has a cylindrical 'blade', so that when it is pushed into the soil, it removes a circular core. Place the bulb at the bottom of the hole, and then crumble the soil removed from the hole back over the bulb and firm it gently. If you are planting into grass, the process is the same, with the circle of turf replaced on top of the crumbled soil.

You can find bulb planters with short, D-shaped, wooden or plastic handles for close use, or with long, T-shaped handles designed for use standing up. Some have hinged blades which open to allow the plug of soil to fall free of the blades more easily.

DIBBERS

The dibber dates back to the mists of gardening history and was originally made from the handle of a broken wooden spade or fork, sharpened to a blunt point. It was ideal for making a small planting hole for transplanting seedlings. Today's dibber may be a straight bar of wood (with or without ornamental turnings) or have a T-, L- or D-shaped handle. The tip

Dibbers and widgers

If you grow a lot of plants from seed, you'll want a dibber or two in your tool kit. Use a narrow dibber (left), also known as a widger, for small seeds and seedlings and a stouter tool (far left) for larger ones or small bulbs.

may be metal to prevent it wearing away, as wooden ones eventually do. Dibbers are ideal for planting out seedlings or plug plants into the garden. For 'pricking out' seedlings, where a finer point is required, slim, plastic dibbers are useful. These often have points at both ends, one smaller than the other.

SIEVES

When you are sowing fine seed, you need the finest possible tilth of soil above and below the seed, so that the seedlings are not overwhelmed. A garden sieve (or 'riddle') will easily allow you to prepare a fine tilth. Once the seed is sown, use the sieve to cover the seedbed with fine particles of soil. It can also be used for sieving topsoil or compost over the lawn to top-dress it. Shake out any stones, twigs or small plants trapped in the mesh, and dispose of these elsewhere.

Sieves have a circular frame of wood, plastic or steel, with the mesh stretched over one side. The mesh varies in hole size, according to the size of particles you want to create. Some models are equipped with interchangeable screens. In order to be fully effective, the soil needs to be moist enough to break up easily, and a quantity placed in the sieve can be pushed through by hand as the sieve is shaken over the area to be covered, so it does not all land in one place.

Sowing seed

1 Fill a seed tray with seed compost. Remove any surplus, then tamp it down very gently. Don't press too firmly or the roots will find it hard to penetrate. Moisten the surface of the soil.

2 Sprinkle the seeds evenly over the soil. If the seeds are very fine, you may need to mix them with dry sand so you can see how much you have sown.

3 Cover the seeds with sieved soil, according to the instructions on the packet, and position the tray so that it receives plenty of light (but not direct sunlight).

4 After germination has occurred, and one or two true leaves have developed, the plants are ready for transferring to another container.

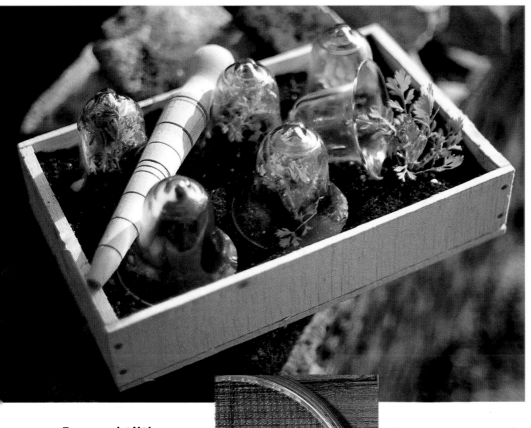

For good tilth

Give your seedlings the best chance of survival by using a sieve to take the lumps out of the soil and put air into it.

PROPAGATING TOOLS

The seeds of many plants are too fragile to sow directly into the ground, in which case you will need to start them indoors.

SEED TRAYS

Get a head start in spring by using seed trays, also known as flats, to grow plants indoors. You can sow them while the weather is still too cold to plant outdoors, and keep them in the protected conditions of the house, greenhouse or cold frame until conditions outside improve. Once they are big enough, you can transplant or 'prick out' the seedlings into separate pots prior to planting outside. Seed trays are usually plastic and rectangular in shape and come in full and half sizes according to the quantity of seed you are sowing. They are reusable once they have been washed clean, and should have drainage holes in the base to prevent waterlogging.

MODULES

These are predivided seed trays that allow you to sow the seed and transplant it some time later without disturbing its roots. When the young plant is ready to transplant, it and its roots can be moved as a block without the need to dig it up. This reduces the chance of it suffering a transplanting shock, which can check growth for a period of weeks. The number of modules per tray varies and can reach up to about 80. They are ideal for growing larger seed (such as runner beans), which can be sown at one or two seeds to each module, or very fine seed (such as lobelia) where a pinch of seeds are sown together, germinate together and will produce a small clump of plants ideal for bedding or display in a hanging basket. You can wash and reuse some plastic trays, others are broken into sections as the plants are removed; some trays are thin and will serve you for one season only.

Flowers by design

There are few more welcoming sights than a carefully crafted cut flower display. Composed in a complementary vase, they make fascinating talking points. But apart from their beauty, there are other reasons for bringing flowers indoors.

Away from the garden where pests, wind, rain and hail can damage opening blooms, buds unfold pristinely and perfectly. Bringing flowers indoors also lets us study their intricate and sensuous shapes. Outdoors, their transient beauty often passes unseen. In a vase, flowers can be admired for days – weeks even.

Arranging flowers is a creative challenge. If you're new to the art form, initial efforts can be a muddle of heights and colours, but as experience grows, you will learn how to associate shapes, textures and colours. You will also discover that certain tools and accessories help to achieve good results.

Cutting tools
First of all, choose a good pair of secateurs that not only slice through stems but grip them too – a big benefit when gathering thorny roses. You will also need them for re-cutting 'tired' ends of woody shoots to expose fresh, water-conducting vessels.

Use a craft knife with a fixed, open blade to cut stem ends – slicing obliquely or splitting – to help them absorb water. Also use it to remove thorns and leaves.

Short-bladed floral scissors, with one serrated blade, are invaluable for cutting stems without crushing them, whereas normal household scissors can damage tissues. There should be ample handle space for fingers and thumb. Most also have a notch for cutting thin wire.

You will need some wire cutters to hand too if you are using chicken wire (as a prop for tall, heavy stems) or thick wire (for supporting dried flowers or for binding blooms so that they form a posy or corsage).

Keeping flowers fresh
A bucket is essential for plunging flowers up to their necks immediately after cutting them. This ensures that the stems are fully charged with moisture. Choose a type with two side-handles, rather than one swinging handle, which may damage your blooms if the handle is not positioned carefully.

Whichever watering can you buy for topping up a vase or rehydrating floral foam, it should be lightweight and have a long thin spout at the base of the can.

Displaying your blooms

A good turntable is invaluable if you are creating an all round (rather than a facing) display. It will save you from constantly lifting the vase to check the height, angle and balance of your flowers and foliage.

Few flower arrangers can do without a little floral foam, soaked and used in a vase to support cut flower stems. Once you have cut it to shape, place this cellular material in the vase or other container. Insert stems into it to hold them firmly at any angle. There are two types of foam: green, which is used in water, and brown or grey.

After soaking green foam in water it absorbs up to 30 times its weight, enabling flowers arranged in it to stay fresher for longer than in water alone. Once wet, green floral foam must not dry out. If you want to use it for several arrangements, wrap it in foil before reusing it. Large displays may need support from chicken wire. Some flowers should not be arranged in foam for they have difficulty absorbing water from it because of their mucilaginous sap. Anemones,

daffodils and tulips are among these and are better displayed in a pinholder (see explanation below).

The other form of floral foam is brown or grey and should be kept dry. Use it to support arrangements of dried or artificial flowers.

Also known as kenzan (a Japanese term literally meaning 'frog pin'), the pinholder is another favourite of flower arrangers. It has a multitude of sharply pointed, circular or rectangular pins that rise from a heavy, ideally brass, base allowing you to insert flower stems between them, ensuring an even, balanced display. Use adhesive clay to stick the pinholder to the base of a vase or bowl. However, a container isn't necessary if you plump for a pinholder with its own water reservoir in the base. Ask for one like this when buying if you'd find it more useful.

Attractive arrangements

To give a display lasting form and structure, wind thin wire around the head and stems of the tallest flowers (centre). Coloured ribbon is ideal for tying bouquets and posies (above). But watch you don't blunt your garden scissors cutting the ribbon – use fabric scissors instead.

WHICH POT IS BEST FOR YOU?

There's no need to take a seedling out of its peat pot when you prick it out, so there is less risk of transplant shock; peat pots can't be reused, however, so are not the best value option.

Plastic pots are light, durable, reusable, and retain moisture well; but they can cause roots to coil up at the base of the pot, which may contribute to transplant shock.

Small metal containers are not cheap but they are attractive and contemporary, making them a good choice if you don't want to transplant the plants.

pot up to the point of planting. Fill each to the brim with compost, insert the plant and water. The peat will soak up water as well as the compost, and a close check should be kept to ensure that they are always moist enough, as moisture evaporates from the sides as well as the top.

Roots will usually start to appear through the sides and base of the pot before the plant is put into its final container, which indicates that the plant is ready to move on. To replant the seedling, make a hole in the ground or in compost in a new container large enough to accommodate the peat pot, and treat the pot as a rootball, covering it over with the new compost.

Plastic pots While diminutive plastic pots may be unsuitable for use in the garden, being unstable in the wind, they make very practical containers for young plants indoors. Durable and recyclable, they don't lose water as quickly as peat pots, but you will need to transplant the plants once they grow too big.

PROPAGATORS

Sometimes seeds and cuttings need a little extra protection to become established and form a good root system. Some plants are particularly fussy and won't grow unless the compost reaches a certain temperature and humidity. In order to meet such requirements, you may need to buy a special case

Modules made of peat have the added advantage that they are degradable, so there is no need to take the plant out of the tray. Simply divide the tray into separate parts and plant the whole module. The roots will grow out through the sides of the module into the soil or compost.

POTS FOR SEEDLINGS AND YOUNG PLANTS

Small containers for small plants come in a variety of materials, including terracotta, metal and the two favourites: peat and plastic. Regardless of the type you choose, always use clean pots and fresh compost.

Peat pots Made of dried, compressed peat, these small containers degrade once they are in the soil or compost, so there is no need to remove the plant from within it as it is planted out. This means less root disturbance, which can halt growth until the plant recovers. They are supplied packed together in an airtight package, and should be treated as any other known as a propagator. These vary from a simple plastic tray with a clear plastic cover designed to keep the air temperature and humidity levels high, to more complex cases with heating cables in the base that warm the compost (rooting zone) as well. The larger cases have a layer of sand in the base over the warming cables, so that there is a residual level of heat to maintain a constant temperature.

The plastic cover should be sturdy and clear to allow as much light through as possible (although you may need to shade the plants if they are growing in bright sunlight). Look for one with a vent you can open to raise and lower the levels of heat and humidity inside, as this will give you much greater control. Wash the cover regularly to prevent algae or fungus from thriving in the moist, warm conditions.

CLOCHES AND COLD FRAMES

Young plants are vulnerable to the cold, particularly if they have been started off indoors. The answer is to use a cloche or cold frame, which shelters plants from the elements. The added warmth and protection from wind, frost, birds and insects will enable you to set out tomatoes, lettuces and other young plants a couple of weeks earlier in the season than you could in open ground; ripen crops such as strawberries more speedily; and extend the growing season.

A cloche is a dome-shaped cover, named after the French word for 'bell', designed to warm the soil for early planting or to protect the plants underneath from the weather. Victorian cloches were like miniature greenhouses, with glazed panels, or bell-shaped glass domes; some could be ventilated, others had to be removed to allow air to circulate. These types of glass cloche are still available today, but plastic varieties are just as effective. Mini versions are excellent for seedlings. Alternatively, you can use plastic sheeting to form a low tunnel over wire hoops, with the ends and sides buried into the soil.

Larger than cloches, cold frames are traditionally wooden-framed structures with glass roofs that keep the light and warmth in. Versions are also available in lighter-weight materials. The roof is usually hinged, so you can increase the ventilation when necessary.

SUPPORTING YOUR PLANTS

Plants need staking to prevent them being damaged by wind, either directly (as the wind causes the shoots to hit each other or a solid object) or indirectly (when the movement of the plant backwards and forwards in the soil loosens the rootball, breaks the roots and makes the plant unstable).

Keep small or thin plants in place using bamboo canes of various lengths and thicknesses. Push the cane into the soil next to the plant and secure the stem to it using twine, raffia or plastic ties. It is important to check these ties regularly or they may begin to cut into the stem as it expands. If this

Bamboo canes, wooden pea sticks and slim plastic stakes make great props for seedlings and small plants. Larger shrubs, trees and climbers will need sturdier supports, such as a metal or wooden stake.

■ You prefer to have plants such as herbs close to the kitchen.
■ You like the flexibility offered by container gardening: shift pots around to highlight changes or move delicate plants to protected spots.

Don't forget that plants in pots require quite a bit more TLC than those growing in the ground: they need regular watering and feeding, especially in the growing season.

CHOOSING CONTAINERS

Pots come in an enormous variety of prices, sizes and also materials, ranging from the traditional terracotta and stone to plastic, reconstituted stone, concrete, wood, metal, rubber and fibreglass.

Be sure to match the size of the container to the size of the plant. The rootball should fit comfortably into the pot, with some space to expand. Large containers retain moisture more efficiently, which is an important point to consider as soil in pots tends to dry out much more quickly than it does in the ground. On the other hand, large containers are difficult to manoeuvre, especially once they have been filled.

Weight is another consideration, particularly if your garden is on a balcony or roof. Pots become much heavier when they are watered, so check out that the structure of your roof or balcony can support the extra weight.

Your choice of shape and style will be a matter of taste. Broadly speaking, traditional urns and decorative pots will suit a formal garden; simple styles will complement a more modern design. Think, too, about the type of plants you wish to place in the container. If they are likely to trail over the sides of the container, hiding most of it from view, then it barely matters what the pot is made of, but if you are growing a slow-growing subject, such as a cactus, you may wish to choose a more attractive container. You could always customize old containers – for instance, a plain metal bucket can be transformed with a verdigris paint finish.

happens, the stem will break at that point the next time it is put under any stress. Canes can be used to guide climbing plants to their permanent growing frame and support lighter plants and flowers.

Larger plants and trees will need a more substantial wooden stake to help them establish after planting. At this time, they are particularly susceptible to wind-rock until the roots have anchored into the soil. A short stake, driven into the soil next to the rootball and tied to the tree at the base, will keep the roots still enough to anchor while allowing the trunk to flex and thicken as it should. By the time the wooden stake rots, the tree should be able to withstand high winds.

A trellis provides a surface for climbing plants to cling to and can be used to divide areas of the garden. Plastic trellis is available, but wooden versions tend to be more popular; both come in a variety of colours.

Other supports for your plants include wigwams, obelisks, arches and pergolas. These may be of bamboo, willow, hardwood, pressure-treated softwood and metal.

POTS AND CONTAINERS

There are many reasons why you might want some plants to live permanently in a container rather than in the ground:

■ You have a balcony, terrace, window box, patio, deck, steps or roof garden that would benefit from a splash of colour.
■ The soil in your garden is unsuitable for certain species; containers are the perfect solution as you can fill these with compost specially suited to particular plants.

Container gardening

Choose pots with a wide base that are stable in the wind. Narrow-necked urns may look fabulous, but you'll find it difficult to re-pot the plants within. Frostproof containers are essential if you live in a cold-winter area.

Terracotta pots look pleasing, are porous (meaning excess moisture can drain away), and allow air to circulate around the roots of the plant. On the minus side, they are easily broken and lose a considerable amount of moisture through their sides, so that you have to water the plants more often. Some are also susceptible to frost damage.

Plastic pots can be washed and reused, and don't need quite so much watering. They are available in a wide range of sizes, from tiny to huge, and are relatively inexpensive. They are ideal for outdoor plants as the intermediate and temporary stage between the seed tray and the final position. But they are more liable to topple over in the wind than their terracotta cousins, and can become brittle when in direct sunlight.

Wood makes a lovely material for containers, but check that the pot is made from hardwood or pressure-treated softwood: otherwise it is liable to rot.

Stone is frostproof and very attractive, but tends to be expensive, so reconstituted stone is a more affordable option. Both can be very heavy.

Metal, and especially galvanized steel, is a popular choice in the contemporary garden. But bear in mind that metal is an efficient conductor of heat, so the soil inside can be poorly insulated. Fibreglass containers are available in a variety of colours, and are durable and lightweight.

SOIL TESTING

The type of soil in your garden will affect how well particular plants will grow. For example, some plants, such as rhododendrons, camellias, and heathers, thrive in acid conditions, whereas others, including dianthus and thyme, do better in alkaline soils. To find out the pH (or level of acidity/alkalinity) of your soil, you will need a soil testing kit.

Testing kits are inexpensive and available at most garden stores. To test one area, take a sample from about 15 cm down into the soil, and use a funnel or piece of paper to pour the soil into the testing bottle. Add water following the manufacturer's instructions, shake and check the results against the colour chart supplied. A pH level of 6.5–7 is regarded as neutral; below neutral is acid, above it is alkaline. To test the whole garden, you can get a representative sample by taking 5 or 6 small amounts from the same depth around the garden and mixing them together. If you find that your soil is unsuited to a favourite plant of yours, you can grow it in a container instead, filled with the appropriate type of compost.

6

Tidying the Garden

A clean sweep

The more efficiently you tidy your garden, the more time you will have to enjoy it. And that's what gardening is: a blend of satisfaction and happy exercise that comes from growing plants to the best of your ability. Many tools have been developed to assist cleaning – from brushes for paths and drives, electric leaf collectors and blowers, and time-saving devices to rationalize your efforts when breaking down prunings.

BROOMS

These are vital for keeping hard surfaces of the garden tidy. There are two main types: besoms and push brooms. The besom is a bundle of twigs wired to a handle and used with a sideways sweeping action. The more popular push broom has a head of bristles with a texture ranging from soft to extra stiff. Handles are replaceable whether they are hardwood (usually ash), heavy-duty plastic or aluminium. The broom is named after a small, wild shrub (of the same name) with butterfly-shaped, yellow pea flowers.

BESOM BROOMS

These are among the oldest tools conceived by humans. Our cave-dwelling ancestors used bunches of twiggy branches to tidy their living quarters. Today

Time to brush up

The besom brush is ideal for clearing autumn leaves and other debris from your lawn. You can also gently remove worm casts from the grass with a besom.

they are made by tightly fixing birch or heather twigs with a wire and metal strap to a stocky pole. They are used for sweeping leaves and bulky litter from paths and patios, or gently teasing fallen twigs and leaves from among border plants. A well-made besom, with plenty of brush like a fox's tail, is a pleasure to use and lasts for years. When not in use, it's best stored upside down to stop the brush head from becoming misshapen.

PUSH BROOMS

There are several versions of the conventional push broom which you stand behind and gently push. Use a soft-bristled head for collecting fine, dusty debris around the house, in a shed or workshop. Opt for a stiffer, springy, bristled head for collecting twigs and other large debris from a patio, path, drive or garden. Bristles are made from hard-wearing natural fibres, PVC or polypropylene. If you have a large area to sweep and need a reliable broom that won't let you down, opt for one that has a reinforced handle with a metal brace for extra stability.

Patio brooms These have short and stocky heads, around 25 cm long, with soft, medium or stiff bristles. Garden brooms are wider and equally versatile. Usefully, some brooms have a dual-handle slot allowing you to move the handle from one side of the

The right broom for the job

The bristles of push brooms (above left) come in different densities – the stiffer they are the larger the debris they will pick up; hand brushes (centre) are perfect for sweeping sand into cracks in the lawn; choose an American shaker brush (right) for sweeping your patio or deck.

head to the other when the bristles wear down unequally. To keep the lawn and patio free from rubbish with one tool, use a combined PVC lawn rake and stiff-bristled broom.

Broom handles The warmest handles are made from wood or plastic-sleeved metal – an important consideration if you are sweeping in winter when bare metal can be exceptionally cold.

Though many brooms come with a wooden handle screwed into the head, some have a useful quick-change system. In this instance, you can replace a

> 'And add to these retired Leisure
> That in trim gardens takes his pleasure'
> JOHN MILTON, POET (1608–1674)

Lawn and leaf rakes

A mini or hand fan rake (left) has a short handle and is perfect for collecting unwanted material from around particular plants; the small sweep rake (centre) has round, flexible tines and a longer handle; expanding varieties (right) enable you to adjust the span of the rake to suit your needs.

broom head with a hoe, rake or another tool head (see boxed feature, page 100). Handles are short, medium or long, but an adjustable, telescopic handle is a good idea if more than one person uses the same broom. Further refinements include a T-shaped handle for precise control of the broom around delicate edging plants.

Prolong the life of your broom by storing it on its handle to avoid distorting bristles, and preserve wooden handles by coating them with linseed oil if they start to look or feel dried out.

FAN RAKES

Autumn leaves are likely to scatter attractively in your garden from the first winds of late summer, but ignore them at your peril. Harbouring potential pests and diseases, they should be cleared up regularly before wintry rains turn them into sludge. Collect them from between border plants, from the surface of your lawn and from under shrubs and hedges for composting into a useful mulch.

The ideal tool for this task is the fan or leaf rake, which differs from the garden rake (page 31) in that its tines are arranged in a fan shape. Use it much as you would a conventional rake for pulling leaves, twigs or grass clippings from amongst plants.

For closely planted beds at ground level or raised beds and borders, it's best to use a flexible model. It can be short- or long-handled, with steel or plastic tines, but it should not be too wide as flared rakes are liable to damage shoots and buds.

Whichever type you select, use it carefully to avoid damaging tines because, when misaligned, these can be difficult to rectify. Lubricate metal parts regularly to keep rust at bay.

SMALL FAN RAKE

A variant of the standard fan rake, the mini version has many virtues. A short, contoured handle ensures a firm grip and reduces slipping, and its nine thin, flat, springy, steel tines are designed to caress the soil and remove debris without harming plants. It's neither too heavy nor too lightweight, and while you work with it you can assess your plants' general health.

SMALL SWEEP RAKE

The comb-like small sweep is a rake you can rely on. Its tines, bent at right angles at the tip, gently prise leaves and other debris from crown buds. To increase its flexibility, use two lengths of handle – a short one for getting in close to plants that need special care, and a longer one for removing litter from the back of a border or from beneath a hedge.

Removing piles of debris

Long-handled metal grabbers (inset) allow
you to remove garden refuse without
bending down; hand grabbers are just as
efficient, but you do need to reach down.

EXPANDING RAKE

This is a voracious rake with a catchment area ranging
from 30 to 48 cm. Its 22 tines slot easily into a semi-
circular adjuster which you can slide up or down to
expand or contract the fan, depending on the size of
the area you are clearing and the type of material you
wish to tackle.

GRABBING RAKES

Transferring the heaps of raked leaves, grass mowings,
hedge trimmings and other rubbish to a cart presents
further choices. The easiest method is to grip the
debris between two rectangular boards and lift it into
the barrow. However, this entails bending, which may
be a problem if you have a weak back. A better
solution is to buy a purpose-made leaf collector made
from galvanized steel. One model looks like a pair of
giant sugar tongs with aligned jaws that cleanly pick
up the smallest heap of rubbish. Another type has
large, toothed, polypropylene jaws which you open
and close around the heap. To maintain, clean the
metal-jawed version with a wooden spatula to remove
caked mud, and spray with lubricant before storing.

One leaf collector looks like a giant pair of baseball
gloves. Made from heavy-duty plastic, with toothed
jaws, it comes with hand-fastening straps. You will, of
course, have to bend to use it – but regular bending
tones up stomach muscles.

BLOWERS AND VACUUMS

You can convert the autumn chore of leaf-collecting
into a short and pleasurable task by using a blower
(which hurls leaves into heaps for collecting later) or a

Outdoor hoovering

Blow autumn leaves into a large pile, then
change the setting and suck the leaves up,
ready for disposal.

vacuum (which sucks leaves into a large pouch). Place all collected leaves into a barrow, then straight onto the compost heap to make useful leaf mould.

Some blowers are easily converted into leaf collectors at the flick of a switch or by fitting a vacuum tube attachment. Leaves sucked into the vacuum pass through a robust steel rotor blade that shreds them before they are packed into a leaf collector bag. When the bag is full, compost the shredded leaves or spread them as a mulch on your shrub and perennial borders.

A blower or powered leaf collector is a sound investment if you have a big garden or large areas of gravel (which makes raking very difficult). But be selective before buying: compare models and ask for a demonstration of both electric and petrol versions. Of the two, a petrol-powered machine is more powerful and versatile – you don't have to negotiate obstacles

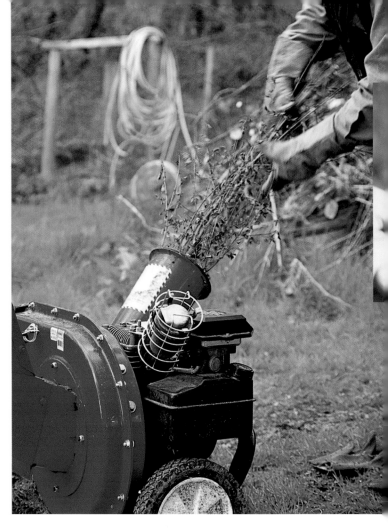

For the pruning season
A shredder is one of the speediest ways of disposing of clippings and prunings. The neatly shredded waste is ready for the compost heap or can be collected for easy disposal. Some models can be fitted with a collecting bag.

MULTI-FUNCTIONAL TOOLS

If space in your garden shed is short, consider investing in a multi-purpose tool. This consists of a special handle onto which you can attach a whole variety of tool heads, including large and small rakes, hoes, brushes, cultivators and so on. Handles are generally available in a range of sizes, from very long to shorter ones suitable for hand tools. These allow you to choose the right model for your height.

and you can use it anywhere without worrying about a power cable. You will need to refill the fuel tank, though, so keep fuel in reserve and store it in an approved container. On the other hand, electric blowers are much quieter, making them a better choice if noise is an issue. Some blowers are very heavy, so be sure you can manoeuvre the tool with relative ease.

If you have a very large area to clear, consider a petrol-powered, back-pack vacuum. These have comfortable harnesses to reduce shoulder load, and rubber damping muffs to absorb engine vibration. There is little maintenance involved provided you keep the machine free from mud, lubricate moving

Small or large?

Many shredders allow you to adjust the cutting size. Fine shreds (left) make ideal mulch for your borders; use coarser shreds (right) in your compost or for mulching larger areas.

parts, spray metal areas with a water-repelling oil and store the machine in a dry place. Drain the petrol tank at the end of the season.

There are few more exasperating sights than a carefully gathered heap of leaves flying away in the wind before you have had a chance to gather it, so use your blower on a windless day or with the wind behind you. A word of warning, though: keep it well away from your delicate plants. It discharges air at over 160 km per hour (100 miles per hour) and can badly batter any plants it meets.

SHREDDERS

Pruning your shrubs and trees is a necessary and very satisfying business. But disposing of the cuttings can be time-consuming – which is where garden shredders come in. These machines make quick work of breaking down twigs and branches into much smaller, more manageable shreds that you can then transfer to your compost bin. They can also reduce autumn leaves into leaf mould, which you can use as a mulch on your beds and borders.

Shredders range from smaller models, which will handle branches up to 3 cm in diameter, to large ones which can take branches of up to 8 cm. Electric models are useful if you have a medium to large garden, though if you have a lot of thick branches to tackle, consider hiring a petrol-powered machine. When choosing a model to hire or buy, look for one that is stable in use; has a safety switch and cut-out in case of blockage; and a means of freeing blockages (such as reverse motion). Finally, consider your neighbours: choose a shredder with a quiet motor if you live in a built-up area.

Most models are very easy to use: simply feed the woody prunings or leaves into a large funnel at one end of the machine, and the shredded material will exit from a chute at the other. Most garden rubbish is suitable for the shredder: vegetable waste, autumn leaves, prunings, hedge, shrub and rose clippings, and even hay and straw. But before you feed material through the shredder, check that there are no stray stones or soil, as these can blunt the cutting blades or block the machine.

Small pieces of wood or twig can sometimes escape at high speed, so always wear eye goggles and thick gloves. Ear protection is also recommended. You'll probably find that the machine clogs up from time to time; remember to disconnect the power and wait for the moving parts to stop before trying to fix it.

'A garden has a curious innocent way of consuming cash while all the time you are under the illusion that you are spending nothing.'

ESTHER MEYNELL, WRITER AND BIOGRAPHER

Water features

Water adds a completely new dimension to a garden – bringing with it life, light, colour and movement. Whether you have in mind a quiet pool or a trickling fountain, there are assorted tools to help create and maintain your garden oasis.

Water gardens are irresistible and endlessly versatile. Even the smallest garden pool invites children and adults to peer into its mysterious depths. Spouts and fountains add sparkle and splash to their surroundings, while quiet pools also have their own serene romance, reflecting the sky, rippling in the breeze and teeming with wildlife.

Design

Water features can take almost any shape or form you choose, from cutting edge, contemporary designs to the most traditional and formal. There are plenty of starter kits and self-contained water features available, which make installing a simple pond or trickling fountain an easy project, or you could use any waterproof materials that take your fancy to make one – such as the watering can shown, far right. Or try adding your own creative touches – perhaps some shell or pebble designs, glass chips or underwater lighting.

Pump power

Moving water features need a good pump to propel them. Submersible pumps with a low voltage are generally simple to install. The size will depend upon the height (or lift) that the water reaches above the surface of your feature, and the amount of water that will be flowing through it (the flow rate). A small feature may require a pump with a flow rate of about 550 litres per hour, while a large fountain or spout may need as much as 1200 litres per hour. There are also a variety of hose fittings and connectors available, some fitted with filters, and some able to adjust the flow of water.

Planting

Think carefully about the plants in and around your water feature; try to choose the right combination of

The water works

Dirty-water pumps (far left) will help to clear muddy water, while there is also a wide range of extendible pond-cleaning tools (centre and left), ideal for skimming and cutting back weed, and for removing fish.

Clearing the waters

Pool-cleaning equipment (left and above) varies from the most basic to the most advanced, but a simple skimmer, net or leaf rake is sufficient to keep the surface tidy. If you have to get in, a pair of waders will keep you warm and dry.

and roots to help prevent overgrown and murky ponds, and they have no sharp edges to damage fish.

Liners

Most ponds are made with one of two types of liner – preformed rigid liners, often made in regular shapes and depths, or flexible sheets, which can be used to fit almost any shape. Underlays are recommended as extra insurance for these liners, and repair kits can be bought to fix minor damage.

Clear water

Healthy, clean water is essential for your water feature to look good and for your fish and plants to thrive. You can buy test sets that will measure the acidity, nitrite and ammonia levels.

Filters can be bought to fit onto pumps or to bury alongside your water feature. They may incorporate a built-in UV Clarifier, or this can be bought separately. Ultraviolet light destroys the green single-celled waterborne algae which make garden ponds murky and unattractive As no chemicals are used, there is no danger of pollution or over treatment of the water and sensitive plant and pond life is not affected.

Manual pumps are available to suck up solids such as silt, leaves and fish droppings, and to pump it onto your flowerbeds as fertilizer. You can also buy powered vacuum cleaners, which are expensive, but are wonderful at removing sludge, algae and leaves from large garden ponds. They usually come with a long suction hose to allow you to reach all parts of your pond.

Effective, safe and fully biodegradable, 'Pond Pads' are a natural treatment for algae in ponds of all sizes. They contain lavender stalks and barley straw, which are both effective natural algaecides. Place one in an area of good water circulation. (Pads will float and may be tethered just below the surface with string and a stone). Add another after 4 months, simply leaving the first pad to rot away. They are not recommended in systems without forced water circulation, however, as there may be a shortage of oxygen in the water.

Pond cover nets will also save you work in autumn, when your water may be swamped by a blanket of dropped leaves.

easy-care aquatic plants so the pond becomes largely self-sustaining. Specially designed baskets are handy to plant in, and are often shaped to follow the contours of pools. More flexible, fabric 'aquaplanters' are available, too, which hold in aquatic compost

Tools for transport

Whether you are harvesting fruit and vegetables, building a new garden structure, planting up containers or weeding your borders, you'll need some holdalls and other hauling equipment to help you move materials around your garden.

If you have a small garden, you'll probably get away with a basket, bucket and trug or two, but a wheelbarrow or cart is a must-have for those with large gardens or if you regularly move heavy loads from one part of your garden to another.

WHEELBARROWS

Since the wheelbarrow was invented in China in around AD 200, it has revolutionized the transport of soil, plants and a thousand other things, allowing us to move weights far greater than we could carry by hand. It is simple in design, consisting of little more than a pair of levers fixed to a large wheel.

It is unlikely that you have ever wondered how a wheelbarrow works, but how does it bear a load far greater than you can carry? Most of the weight, when

Holding and hauling

A basket (above) is perfect for moving small, lightweight items around the garden; use a wheelbarrow (right) for bulkier materials.

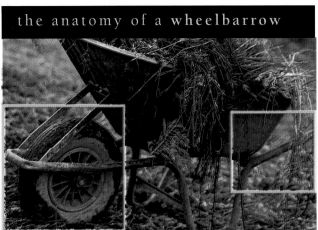

Look for a barrow with a pneumatic tyre, at least 10 cm wide, which will absorb shocks without jolting and which rides comfortably over a bumpy surface; a frame of reinforced tubular steel; a deep, high-capacity steel or polypropylene tray; and a projecting metal 'nose' to make tipping easier.

you lift the handles, is transferred to a wheel that acts as a fulcrum. Indeed, the mass pressing down on the wheel actually aids forward movement. With just one wheel, the wheelbarrow is extremely manoeuvrable. It allows you to twist, turn and negotiate obstacles, even along narrow paths.

The first wheelbarrows designed for gardens were heavy, wooden carts with metal-rimmed wheels. These barrows never wore out, but what a noise they made when trundled over uneven stone or concrete surfaces. You can still buy old-fashioned wooden barrows, but you may prefer a modern, lighter version. Whatever you use your wheelbarrow for – shifting manure, soil, weeds, stones, logs, leaves, grass cuttings, prunings or bags of cement – it's vital to load it on a level surface. You can double the capacity of some models by fitting an extension top. This is invaluable for collecting leaves in the autumn.

To keep your wheelbarrow in peak working order, wipe the tray out each time you use it – you may need to use a wire brush if mud is really caked on – and up-end the barrow to drain it. Lubricate the wheel fittings once a season and check all the nuts and screws on a yearly basis, tightening if necessary. It is also worth pumping up the tyre from time to time.

THE HISTORY OF WHEELBARROWS

The wheelbarrow has been around for millennia in China. An inventor called Ko Yu is credited with the idea for the first wheelbarrow, possibly around the first century BC. The invention has been used in China ever since for carrying all manner of items, from agricultural materials and war equipment (the tool was a favourite with ancient Chinese armies) to human beings.

It wasn't until the eleventh or twelfth century AD that the wheelbarrow first appeared in Europe – the earliest known Western depiction is in a window at Chartres Cathedral, France, dated around 1220 AD. Farmers soon discovered that the wheelbarrow was a cheap and efficient substitute for draught animals.

Today, tractors and harvesters are used to do most of the hard work on agricultural land, but the wheelbarrow still has pride of place in the domestic garden shed.

Through the ages

Early models had a wheel in the centre of the wooden frame; later, the wheel was placed at the front of the frame instead. The materials have evolved, too: for centuries wood was favoured for the tray, frame and even the wheel, but gradually this was replaced by longer-lasting metal frames, metal or plastic trays and pneumatic rubber tyres.

Fold-away barrows

Traditional wheelbarrows are quite bulky and take up a lot of storage space. Some manufacturers make a folding wheelbarrow as an alternative. This model has a canvas tray and a lightweight frame, and can be hung from a hook in the wall when not in use.

METAL MODELS

Metal wheelbarrows come in many shapes and sizes, all of which should be stored under cover. Some trays are galvanized; others are made of a reinforced polypropylene tray that's unaffected by temperatures from 70°C to minus 25°C. This material won't dent, buckle or become brittle when frosted.

The strongest frames are wrought from a single length of tubular steel with two welded cross members. When it comes to wheels, choose from solid or tubeless pneumatic tyres (filled with compressed air). For the smoothest ride, buy a wheelbarrow with a broad pneumatic tyre (about 10 cm thick) and 'needle' bearings.

How much a barrow can carry depends on its size. Unless you have weak wrists, don't buy a model with less than 90 litres' capacity. After all, you don't have to fill it so full that you stagger with it. The deeper it is, the more useful it will be to you.

A barrow with a tool box accessory at the base of the handles will provide permanent storage for your secateurs, trowel, string and knife.

FOLDING-FRAMED BARROWS

If you're stuck for space and haven't room for a rigid-framed barrow, opt for a folding version that can be hung on a wall. Sturdy and well-balanced, its galvanized frame supports a deep tray of tough, tear-resistant fabric and a chunky solid wheel takes the strain. It's easy to push when piled high with garden rubbish and as versatile as a conventional barrow; it can even be used for carting logs and bricks.

CARTS AND TROLLEYS

With larger trays or pans than a barrow, carts are well-balanced for moving heavy loads. They are strong enough to withstand rough use year after year and, being two-wheeled, they can't accidentally topple sideways. What's more, the flat bottom makes for easy stacking. They are also simple to empty: just tip them forwards. There are two kinds: one has a bolt-free polyethylene tray that snaps onto and off a tubular,

Garden dollies

Constructed from pine or UV-protected polypropylene, and fitted with hard-wearing castors, plant dollies (right) are the easy and sensible answer to moving weighty patio tubs and pots or bags of compost or cement. Some kinds have enclosed wheel housings for extra strength.

aluminium alloy frame for emptying. The other has a galvanized steel tray; epoxy-coated, tubular steel frame; spoked wheels with bearings; and a large pan.

Four-wheeled trolleys vary in size enormously. One type, made from rugged polypropylene, has a large central compartment, moulded tool clips to hold long-handled tools and an adjustable handle which folds to form a comfortable seat.

SACK TRUCKS

Originally, millers used sack trucks to transport corn and flour, and the name stuck. The big advantage of a sack truck over a cart is that you do not have to lift the load. You simply ease the base plate under the object you wish to lift and pull back on the handles. Most base plates are flat, but some have right-angled sides to stop the load from slipping.

When using a sack truck at a 45 degree angle from the ground, the leverage is such that you can transport exceptionally heavy loads…albeit slowly. Indeed, a

Save your back

For moving really heavy items, such as large containers, a sack truck will come in useful, as you can slide the footplate under the pot instead of lifting the pot onto the truck.

ROLL-OUT PATHWAYS

Walking or transporting loads across rain-drenched lawns and borders in foul weather is totally inadvisable. Wet soil is easily compressed, and its fragile, open structure quickly destroyed. However, you can keep on the move by laying a 30-cm-wide portable path made from tough, interlocking moulded polypropylene slats. It's the sensible way to keep working during showers.

The roll-out pathway has other uses, too. Lay it alongside a row of peas or beans to allow you to pick pods on the wettest day of summer without dirtying your shoes or compacting and damaging soggy soil. When you've finished with it, hose it down, roll it up and store it.

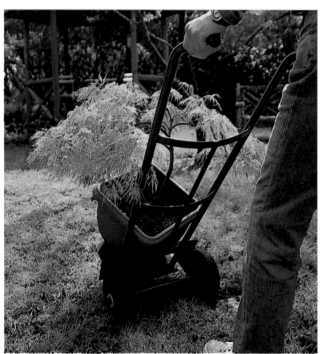

sack truck is ideal for moving large, heavy, planted containers and tubs, rock garden stone, peat bales, and bags of compost, gravel and cement. When you deposit the load, simply ease it forwards slightly to release the base plate.

STEPLADDER TRUCK TROLLEY

This variation on the sack truck is a useful combination of a two-step ladder and truck which saves you looking for a box to stand upon when you need to move out-of-reach objects. An occasional squirt of oil to stop the wheels from squeaking is all you need to remember.

BUCKETS, BAGS AND SHEETS

Whether it's made from galvanized steel, rubber or heavy-duty plastic, a bucket is a gardener's ally when tidying borders. While weeding, it's easy to first fill a bucket with weeds and then empty it into a barrow. A

All-purpose tools

No garden shed is complete without a bucket or two, either of galvanized steel (far left), plastic (left) or even rubber; use them to carry or mix materials.

bucket is also indispensable for mixing fertilizer, baling out a pond and for filling with soap solution to wash dirty pots.

You will find many uses for a capacious bag made from durable, woven polypropylene: have it beside you when weeding a border or pruning shrubs.

A tough, waterproof sheet has similar beneficial uses. Spread it out where you are working in the garden and throw weeds and other rubbish onto it. When full, gather it up and add the contents to your compost bin, fire heap or dustbin.

BUCKETS

As Jeff Taylor says in his book, *Tools of the Earth*: 'No garden can get by without a bucket or three. It is among the most versatile, ignored, and generally abused tools. It gets tossed about and dropped, filled with all sorts of unpleasant things, and left out in the elements. All other garden tools get a spring clean and a winter rest, but never the bucket. It hauls ash from the wood stove to the ash can and fills up with rain or snow in between.'

Whether you prefer a galvanized bucket with a thick, wire handle and double-locked, side seams; a heavy-duty, plastic builder's bucket with a lip for pouring; or one with a rope handle, the heavier the bucket, the less likely it is to be blown around in gusty weather. It's even more useful when calibrated in gallons and litres. If you decide to buy a galvanized steel bucket, examine it closely. Make sure that the handles and base are securely attached to the body, and that the seams are well-sealed and galvanized – for even the smallest holes attract rust. When you've finished using the bucket, store it in a dry place.

Top-quality plastic buckets are lighter than steel but just as strong and rust-free. They also tend to cost much less than their metal counterparts.

BAGS

The choice of bags is enormous: one version, made from strong, waterproof nylon with webbing handles, stands up for filling, but is easily collapsed for storage and transport. A family of garden tidy bags you'll want to become familiar with are made from tough

>good ideas

Attempting to hold a bag open with one hand while you shovel leaves, soil or other debris into it with the other can be a trying experience. So manufacturers have come up with an ingenious design for a self-opening and collapsing bag. While in use, it stays open for easy filling and emptying (you can also angle the bag to make this task even simpler), and when you've finished, it collapses into a neat, flat disc for easy storage and transportation.

Versatile tip sheets

These are perfect for collecting weeds and garden rubbish (above). If you are collecting a lot of material, such as when hedge trimming, sheets are available that join together with bamboo canes (right); once you have finished your task, remove the canes and use the handles at each corner (far right) to gather up the cuttings and dispose of them.

non-tear, woven polyethylene. Some are self-supporting, with a huge capacity; others, which also stand up by themselves, have flexible inserts. Many come with robust nylon handles, and all wipe clean.

A clever hybrid between a barrow and a bag is the refuse cart – a large polyethylene bag supported by a wheeled and galvanized steel frame. Simply fill the bag and wheel it to your compost heap. An extra benefit is that you can consign it to the boot of your car for an unmessy trip to the rubbish dump.

SHEETS

Woven polyethylene sheets are invaluable for collecting weeds and leaf litter while you're immersed in a border. Spread a sheet out on the grass or pathway and throw all your border waste onto it. When you've built up a sizable heap, grab the four carrying handles and fold them into the middle. Dump the contents onto your compost heap.

An attractive alternative to a plastic sheet is a carrier made of heavy-duty, oiled, green canvas. Edged with natural hessian, it is tough enough to cope with most garden waste and less likely to get punctured by a stray twig than the plastic versions. If you're taking a load of rubbish in your car boot to the dump, tie the

handles together. Keep sheets free from mud by hosing them down, drying them and storing them until their next use.

TRUGS

This lovely, old-fashioned word describes long, light, shallow baskets traditionally crafted from veneers of wood. The body is usually made from willow; the handles and trim from sweet chestnut. Generally there are three sizes to choose from. The smallest (60 x 20 cm) is ideal for carrying items like small tools; the next size up (48 x 28 cm) is perfect for kitchen-garden produce; and the largest (63 x 35 cm) is favoured by gardeners who spend many hours in the garden. The shallow cradle of all trugs means that you can carry cut flowers indoors without squashing the delicate flowerheads.

Also known as the tub trug, the two-handled trug is strong, flexible and made from recycled plastic. Use it to gather weeds and other rubbish; to carry plants and tools; to mix compost and to scoop organic matter.

BASKETS

Wicker (willow), bamboo, wire and rush – these lightweight materials make the perfect container for newly harvested fruit, vegetables and, of course, flowers for your table. For carrying heavier crops, use a high-sided wooden or canvas fruit-picker's basket. Wire baskets are handy too as they allow air to circulate around fruit and vegetables, and also are impervious to mould.

THE MAKING OF TRUGS

When harvesting flowers, you need a lightweight, shallow container in which to lay the blooms so that they won't get squashed. The ideal tool for the job is the trug, which was invented in the 1820s by Thomas Smith of Herstmonceux, a village in southern England.

The trug takes its name from an Anglo-Saxon word, 'trog', which was a wooden vessel, shaped like a round coracle boat, used by farmers to measure grain and liquids. Thomas Smith redesigned the historic trog to produce a lighter-weight basket, made of sweet chestnut and willow wood. The trug soon became a favourite of gardeners around the world.

Traditionally made trugs are still available today, in durable chestnut, lightweight willow, plywood, birch veneer and other natural materials such as plaited rush. A well-crafted, handmade trug is a better investment than a plastic imitation: kept dry, it will last for years – and it looks so at home on the kitchen table or in the garden shed.

Handmade trugs

To make traditional Sussex trugs, skilled craftspeople today employ virtually the same techniques as Thomas Smith would have used nearly 200 years ago.

1 CUTTING THE SLATS Lengths of willow are hand-shaved into very fine strips of about 3 mm thick, which will make the slats for the trug.

2 MAKING THE FRAME Pieces of chestnut are cut into lengths for the rim and handle, which are then steamed to make them flexible. Next, the wood is bent around a frame to make a hoop, which is held with small tacks. After the handle and rim have been nailed together, the willow slats are steamed and curved, then nailed to the frame.

3 FINISHING TOUCHES The slats are trimmed down to create a neat edge.

Composting

There are few more satisfying tasks in gardening than converting organic waste into nutrient-rich humus. It's not only free to make and environmentally responsible, but also the soil's life blood. Weeds, grass cuttings, soft prunings, plant remains, peelings and other kitchen waste – whatever you recycle – the end product is similar. If you make an effort to keep it warm, moist and aerated, your reward will be a crumbly, black material teeming with worms and beneficial microbes that is excellent for conditioning your soil. It improves the structure of all soils, opening the texture of heavy clay soils (thereby aiding drainage and root growth), helping sandy soils to retain water and adding vital nutrients. The result is a more productive garden.

To make a compost heap you can simply pile waste green materials into a corner of the garden where they will eventually decompose. But the most efficient way to process green waste is to keep it in a purpose-made compost bin that keeps it under the right conditions in which micro-organisms break it down into humus.

Aim to spend a little time blending fibrous, carbon-rich materials such as dry leaves or straw, which give

COMPOSTING THROUGH THE AGES

It can't have escaped early humans' attention that wherever they emptied their bladders, the vegetation grew exceptionally well. Patches of very lush grassland would crop up where ground was fertilized in this way.

Around 1000 years ago it was common practice to add blood, including that from humans, with dung, wood ash, manure and other rottable materials. In the late 19th century, the almost sanctified habit of composting was eclipsed by the introduction of artificial fertilizers. Thankfully, this short-sightedness was brief and compost heap devotees continued thereafter to perfect their art.

The birth of the 20th century found Sir Albert Howard stating that the best compost is made by mixing three parts plant waste to one part manure. A century later, it's still a highly respected formula.

> 'Everyone has a theory about composting. For the kitchen refuse I keep a big brown pot on the windowsill behind the sink, and into it go all the tea leaves, apple peel, onion skins, and coffee grounds.'
>
> MARGERY FISH, GARDENING WRITER (1888–1969)

your heap 'body', with softer nitrogen-rich waste, such as grass cuttings, fruit and vegetable scraps and old, unwanted garden plants. Keep a healthy balance: if there's too much carbon, compost will take a long time to break down and, conversely, if there's an excess of soft-stemmed material, it will become a slimy, airless mess.

The larger the bin, the more heat it retains and the quicker compost will decompose. If you have enough space, try to keep two adjoining bins: one full with compost left to finish rotting down; and the other in the process of being filled.

COMPOST BINS

Your compost bin should be at least 300 litres in volume with a lid to keep materials warm and actively 'fermenting'. There should also be a door at the base – or a removable side – for digging out well-rotted compost. If there is no door, tilt the bin to remove the finest compost (usually from the bottom of the heap).

Wooden bins These are normally made of preserved softwood panels at least 19 mm thick; the container should not be less than 90 cm square and deep. Some models have interlocking sides to make it easy to remove compost.

Plastic Usually made from recycled heavy-duty polypropylene, plastic is tough and durable and won't crack in sub-zero temperatures or perish when it's hot. Most kinds have wide, easy opening doors, either hinged or sliding, and a full-sized lid for easy filling.

Wire mesh Easy to make, plastic-coated wire mesh is fixed to a framework of four preserved posts. Insulate the bin with polystyrene sheets or thick cardboard to stop drying or chilly winds from cooling the heap.

Plastic fertilizer bags Moist leaves and other finely shredded waste will rot down within these small bags. When full, tie the bag tightly at the top and make a

WHICH COMPOST BIN IS BEST FOR YOU?

When choosing a compost bin, take into account the size and style of your garden. If you have just a compact garden, opt for a small, discrete model; larger gardens can support a bigger bin. Plastic bins (top) retain heat efficiently and are easily transported around the garden. Chicken wire composters (centre) are simple to construct – see overleaf – and a good choice for the budget-conscious. Wooden, interlocking bins (below) may come with a removable front for easy access to the compost.

few ventilation holes in the side with a garden fork. Store the bags in a cool, wind-free part of the garden until the contents have broken down into crumbly black humus and are ready for use.

Compost tumbler This unique device is a plastic bin mounted on a sturdy galvanized-steel frame that you turn daily to force oxygen through the waste. This stimulates microbes to break down organic matter which, in turn, raises the temperature to 50°C and causes compost to decompose rapidly. So in summer, finely shredded organic waste can be converted into humus within as little as five weeks. After processing the compost, you can either spread it around the garden and dig it in, or add it to a compost bin where it will break down into finer particles. A simpler version of the compost tumbler is a big hollow plastic ball with a lid on the top, which you can roll this way and that to keep turning the compost inside.

COMPOSTING MATERIALS

Good compost-making ingredients include fruit and vegetable scraps, straw and hay, spent flowers and bedding plants, soft prunings, pet bedding, tea bags and coffee grounds, vegetable plant remains, young hedge clippings, wood ash, cardboard, paper towels, egg boxes and perennial weeds (apart from persistent horrors such as couch grass and ground elder).

Never compost cat litter, dog faeces, disposable nappies, meat or fish, as these will attract vermin. Glossy magazines, coal and coke ash will not decompose. Also avoid onions infected with white rot, potatoes with blight, brassicas diseased with club root or weeds that have already gone to seed.

TIPS FOR SUCCESS

Activators A compost activator speeds up the rotting process and is usually found in manure, artificial fertilizers, microbes or enzymes. Comfrey leaves, grass cuttings and young weeds will also kick-start beneficial bacteria into breaking down the heap.

Good insulation No matter what sort of compost container you opt for, it must retain heat. Decomposition stops if chilly winds cool 'fermenting'

Making a simple compost bin

1 Using a large, heavy mallet or hammer, drive four sturdy fence posts into the ground to form a square. These will help to stabilize the bin.

2 Wrap galvanized chicken wire around the posts. You'll need about 3.5 metres of 90-cm-wide, 3-cm wire mesh to make a container 1 metre in diameter. Non-galvanized wire is less weather-resistant and won't last as long.

3 Fold back 8 or 10 cm at each end of the wire, to make a clean edge that won't easily snag.

4 Secure the wire to the posts with nails. Fold the nail back on itself, using a hammer, for extra strength.

5 Attach the two ends of the chicken wire together using some heavy wire. You may need pliers for this job.

6 To remove the finished compost, simply disconnect the wire on one side of the bin. Alternatively, for even easier access, consider constructing a gate on one side of the bin.

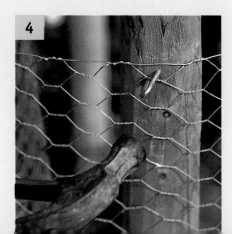

Green gardening

Composting is central to organic gardening. Other eco-friendly practices include installing a lacewing chamber (right), which helps these beneficial insects overwinter safely. You can also encourage mason wasps – essential for pollinating fruit trees – to live in your trees with a specially designed shelter (far right) and nesting tubes.

compost. A thick sheet of polystyrene is one of the most efficient insulators – in fact some compost bins are made from it! It's usually sandwiched between two layers of heavy-duty plastic to prevent the polystyrene from cracking. Tough polypropylene or wooden panels, not less than 19 mm wide, also keep heat where you want it – breaking down plant tissue.

Positioning the bin Warmth and moisture are absolutely vital for making good garden compost, so position the container in a sheltered spot where icy winds cannot cool it. There should also be room next to it for a barrow, and for stacking materials before you load them into the bin. Choose a well-drained area of soil for the bin to sit on, as you want worms and microbes to enter the heap. You may also want to position your bin so that you cannot see it from the windows of your house.

Maintain the decomposition process You should aim to turn your pile about once a month to speed the natural breakdown of the organic matter. If you don't turn it regularly, the composting process will slow down and you may notice an unpleasant smell beginning to emanate from your pile. (For details on how to tend your compost pile, see below.)

A standard, four-tined garden fork will do an adequate job of turning your pile, but you will find a compost or manure fork more helpful as the five or six more closely spaced tines grab onto the plant material with greater efficiency and less will escape from between the prongs.

The enthusiastic compostor might like to consider investing in an aerator (a blade at the end of a long handle) which helps to introduce oxygen to the pile, and a special long compost thermometer which allows you easily to take temperature readings at the centre of the pile.

CREATING A COMPOST HEAP

Start by covering the base with a 10-cm layer of coarse prunings or brassica stems to help air circulate through the heap. Add a 20-cm layer of mixed coarse and fine waste. Avoid thick slabs of grass which exclude air and turn smelly. Cover the compost with a granular or liquid activator. Water dry materials or they won't rot. Continue in this fashion, adding 20-cm layers of compost treated with activator, until you have filled the container. Throughout this period, keep the lid on to stop rain from soaking the compost and arresting its breakdown.

Within a week or so, the heap will heat up. When it cools, turn materials with a fork. Aim to work the cooler and less decomposed outside of the heap into the middle. When the heap reheats, air introduced when mixing materials will stimulate microbes to continue feasting. Turn the heap again. Finally, when it no longer heats up, leave it to finish composting.

You will know the decomposition process is complete and the compost is ready to use when you have a rich, crumbly brownish black material. Add a 3- to 5-cm layer of compost to your flower beds each year to keep the soil healthy and fertile. It also makes a good mulch around newly planted flowers and shrubs, and an efficient fertilizer for your lawn. When using compost on your borders, you may want to sift it first with a garden sieve to remove any larger, undecomposed debris.

7

Working Safely

Protective clothing

Do you mind what you wear when you are gardening? Probably not – provided you are comfortable, your clothes are loose and you can bend and twist without getting caught up. Few of us actually buy gardening clothes. Instead we tend to recycle old shirts, jumpers and long trousers that have lost their respectability. When you're digging in manure, weeding or planting, it's only your neighbours who can see you and they are probably similarly attired. However, some items of clothing should not be worn when old and worn out, such as boots, gloves, waterproof jackets, fleeces and hats. And some items should never be worn when gardening because they can get caught up in equipment: these include jewellery and loose-fitting clothes. Untied long hair can also be hazardous.

But no matter how experienced a gardener you are, you should be aware of the elements to which you are exposed when gardening. On a day-to-day basis, you will need to evaluate how best to protect yourself from a panoply of hazards. These may include exposure to the burning effects of the sun; the unpleasant dampness of the rain; the risk of contact with insects and irritant plants; and the cuts and bruises you may receive through using your tools.

Before starting a job, think carefully about what clothing and footwear you will need to accomplish it safely. You should always protect your eyes with safety glasses when mowing, pruning, trimming hedges and using a chain saw. Similarly, safeguard your hands with thornproof gloves when pruning hooked rose stems. Wear long-sleeved gloves for rearranging water plants in ponds and strap-on kneeling pads to cushion your knees from sharp stones or damp.

'Oh, Adam was a gardener, and God who made him sees
That half a proper gardener's work is done upon his knees'

RUDYARD KIPLING, NOVELIST AND POET (1865–1936)

LOOKING AFTER YOUR FEET

Never wear old shoes in the garden as their soles are likely to be thin and won't offer much in the way of protection, as they are easily punctured by nails, thorns and other sharp objects. Wounds can then become infected with tetanus – for which you should be regularly immunized.

Unless your shoes are made of tough leather or rubber, they are unlikely to be waterproof, and wet feet are not only unpleasant but may cause you to suffer from a host of ailments. To garden comfortably, hour after hour, you will need two sorts of boots: Wellingtons, and boots made from leather, rubber or PVC. Your choice of which to wear will depend on the day's activities and the tools you intend to use.

WELLINGTON BOOTS

These are ideal for short periods of muddy work in wet spells when lawns and borders are saturated. They should fit snugly around your feet and legs and have reinforced soles to protect your feet from the sharp edge of a blade when you are digging or using implements like lawn edgers.

If you're working for several hours, short-length Wellingtons are better than full-length ones, which may rub your legs and make them sore. If you wade into a pond wearing Wellingtons, check frequently that the water level is below the top of your boots – there's nothing worse than damp feet!

Long PVC or rubber Wellingtons should be lined for comfort and have reinforced seams for strength and a cushioned sole. Some have a steel shank for added support and an adjustable strap at the top. There are several types: one very popular form, if you suffer from cold feet, is a snug-fitting PVC boot. Plain-styled with a square toe, it has a textile-ribbed or padded rubber and laced collar and comes complete with a textile inner lining which will keep your feet warm during icy spells.

CLOGS, SHOES AND ANKLE BOOTS

Very convenient and easy to wear, waterproof clogs, slip-on shoes and ankle boots are best used for brief dashes into the garden. Keep them by the back door for wearing when nipping out to empty the rubbish, feed the birds or pop into the garden shed.

Mud, mud, glorious mud

Wellington boots really come into their own when the ground is wet. Look for a high-grip tread pattern to provide a better slip-free foothold.

Out to dry

At the end of the day, hang your mucky boots on a boot rack. Brush off the caked mud once it has dried.

Natural rubber clogs are reliable and enjoyable to wear, especially if they have cork insoles and cotton lining to absorb perspiration. A reinforced area under the ball of the foot makes digging a painless exercise. Incidentally, over rough ground, closed-backed clogs are easier to keep on than open-backed ones.

If you intend to spend only few moments on a saturated lawn or border, you can put on overboots rather than Wellingtons. Strong, waterproof and easily slipped on over shoes, they are made from natural latex and have reinforced soles.

LEATHER AND PVC BOOTS

Whether they are made from leather or PVC, boots are more comfortable than basic Wellingtons and can be worn for longer periods without 'drawing' your feet. If you have a largish garden in which you spend a lot of time walking from one job to the next, a strong, waterproof pair of boots is essential, particularly if you have uneven patches of ground in your plot over which you could stumble.

When buying full-grained, lace-up leather boots (which have a very long life), make sure they have thick and hard-wearing soles to cushion you against sharp stones, nails and other objects. They should also have a moisture-wicking liner (which removes perspiration from your feet), a flexible but tough mid-sole and a lightweight carbon-rubber outsole.

Alternatively, opt for lightweight 'breathable' boots made from suede and waterproof Gore-Tex. Steel toe caps are not necessary unless you are cutting heavy branches which might land awkwardly. Another type of waterproof boot has PVC soles and Velcro fastenings – so you can take them off much more quickly than you can untie boot laces.

Should you need to work in deep water, slip on a pair of medium-weight thigh-, waist- or chest-length PVC waders. Textile-lined, they come with a reinforced ankle, heel and toe.

CHEST, ARMS AND LEGS

You must not forget, when tackling a multitude of gardening challenges, to respect the weather and dress accordingly. To enjoy these tasks, it's vital that you stay snug and warm during rain and chilly winds – while feeling cool when the sun heats the garden.

Slip-ons

Natural rubber clogs (right) are easy to step into and out of when you're coming and going from the garden. Overboots (far right) are also good for running in and out of the house.

Keep your clothes clean by wearing an apron over the top (far left); pockets are a handy place to stash hand tools and other accessories when not in use. Knee pads (left) will cushion your delicate knee joints and also prevent slipping.

Sweat – inevitably produced by vigorous exercise – should not build up. If it does, and you stop working, it may 'ice' the skin and trigger aches and pains. It's important to wear clothes that 'wick away' moisture immediately. That means using a three-layer system.

First layer Worn next to the skin, Polartec – based on polyester – absorbs less than half of one per cent of its weight of water. Close-fitting shirts and trousers in this material are a pleasure to wear, pulling moisture away from your body, to leave it warm and dry.

Second layer This consists of a fleecy, high-loft garment which not only traps warm, dry air close to your body, but allows moisture to evaporate. Most fleeces have a high double collar, front pockets and draw-string hem with locking toggle.

Third layer This top layer should be a jacket made from breathable but waterproof and windproof Gore-Tex which retains body heat but allows body water vapour to escape. Make sure that the version you buy has taped seams, articulated elbows for easy movement, a peaked roll-away hood with side drainage channels, adjustable outer cuffs and large pockets. It should also be machine washable.

Aprons Why soil a shirt or trousers with potting compost or other staining substances when you can wear an apron to keep yourself clean and warm on a cool day? Knee-length, bib-types are best, made of polyester and cotton, or denim with one or more large pockets for carrying string and secateurs.

Waders and garden boots

If you have a large pond in your garden (or are partial to fishing), you may want to invest in a pair of thigh-length waders (far left). Oiled, leather boots (left) are generally built to last; this particular pair is slip-on, which saves on endless lacing and unlacing.

Child's play

Encouraging a budding young gardener to develop his or her creative talents is a joyous duty, and one made much easier and safer by some of the purpose-designed tools that are available today.

It's heartening when a child – curious and interested in what you're doing in the garden – wants to join in and help.

The first step is to give the budding gardener a well-drained plot on which to grow anything that appeals – from showy sunflowers and nasturtiums to perennials, vegetables and fruit. Thankfully, a few enterprising companies have designed good, lightweight tools for children, which should not break if they are misused. It's probably best to avoid giving youngsters adult-sized spades, forks, hoes or rakes, as these will be too large and heavy, and may prove hazardous.

Safe digging tools

Initially, it's a good idea for an adult to dig the patch of ground to make it easier for the child to cultivate. But then there is a variety of tools to help youngsters to take over.

Few garden tasks are more riveting for a child than planting perennials and bedding plants that grow and flower quickly, for them to see. Make this easy with a tough, plastic, well-designed hand fork.

You can also plant bulbs with a hand fork, but it's easier to set them with a trowel. Mark the blade in centimetres so the child knows exactly how deep to dig a hole for small or large bulbs.

The best spades – which can also be used as shovels – have durable fibreglass-reinforced plastic, shield-shaped blades with wooden pole-shaped handles.

Learning the fun way

Setting your children projects with rewarding outcomes – such as proudly eating their own produce or enjoying fast-growing annual flowers – will fire their imaginations.

Kitting out

Clockwise from left: equip your kids with colourful Wellingtons, preferably with reinforced seams and, crucially, a high-grip tread; there are kids' versions of most adult tools, including rakes, brooms, spades, wheelbarrows and watering cans.

Clean and rake it up

Essential for levelling and crumbling soil, and covering seedlings, there are heavy-duty plastic and fibreglass rakes with 10 tines and wooden handles. You can also buy children's leaf rakes, replicating in miniature a flexible 12-tined adult version. The fibreglass and plastic teeth effectively aerate a lawn by teasing clogging thatch from grass blades.

It is also worth buying a broom, so your child can enjoy sweeping clean a path, patio or terrace. Choose a stiff-bristled model with small head and short handle.

To help children develop a passion for gardening, do stress the fun aspect – and that means buying a lightweight barrow and offering them a ride in it! One of the best has a dashing, red-painted 25-litre tray on a matt-black frame. It runs well, thanks to a polypropylene wheel and safety-grip handles which help you balance the load.

It is also worth remembering that grown-up watering cans are too heavy for youngsters: the ideal size is a 1-litre can.

Plantings

The faster seeds germinate, the more they can hold a child's attention. Buy a mustard and cress hedgehog with a hollow back, fill it with compost and moisten it. Sprinkle mustard seeds thickly over the compost and sow the cress three days later. Mist seeds. Place the hedgehog in a clear plastic bag and move it to a warm, dark place. When, after a week or so, seedlings are 5 cm high, transfer them to a sunny spot to green up.

In early autumn, buy prepared hyacinth bulbs. Set them almost touching in bowls of bulb fibre. Water them in and put in a cool, dark place to form roots. When after six weeks or so, leaves are 3–5 cm high with embryo blooms showing, move to a sunny spot.

Mark rows of plants with labels in the form of snails, hedgehogs and bees to fuel a child's enthusiasm.

PROTECTING YOUR HANDS

Without gloves to guard us from icy winds that numb fingers and crack skin, gardening would not be the pleasant, comfortable pastime it is. Besides comfort, they do a very good job of protecting us from cruel rose thorns and manure that often harbours tetanus.

There are waterproof gloves to keep us warm and dry; woollen mitts that cover all but finger tips; tough thornproof gauntlets for tackling vicious shrubs; and long-sleeved versions for dabbling in ponds.

THE GLOVE TEST

All gloves should be strong enough to withstand repeated encounters with an enemy of barbed shrubs and stony soil. They should also be flexible and sensitive enough for us to carry out nimble tasks. We tend to buy gloves for different purposes: light weeding; handling rough objects; pruning; and keeping dry when it's wet.

FABRIC GLOVES

Cotton, jersey and canvas gloves are inexpensive and ideal for keeping hands clean on a dry day – as hands can also breathe – but the best have PVC dots for a better grip. Look for a clute-cut glove in which the palm side is a single piece of material. Fabric gloves are machine washable at 40°C. If you wear them when it's wet they soak up water and your hands will freeze.

VINYL GLOVES

These are hard-wearing and waterproof but sufficiently flexible and close fitting for sowing seeds or taking cuttings. Vinyl gloves have a warm, soft cotton lining and they won't clog with dirt.

STORING GLOVES SAFELY

When you have finished using them, make a habit of storing them in the same place every time. Coming in pairs, it's exasperating to lose one: you won't do this if you buy a brand that can be snapped together when not in use. They will serve you well as long as you wash them occasionally to remove the dirt that tends to accumulate in the finger tips. When dry, store them flat in a warm, dry place. Never stuff them in pockets, which will ruin their shape.

THE FINER POINTS...

Seamless...
Choose gloves that have a flexible, seamless back. They should be comfortable and roomy – too tight and they will restrict blood flow and your fingers will stay cold.

Leather-palmed...
These should have a safety cuff for extra wrist protection.

Double sewn thumbs...
Ensure that tough, hard-wearing gloves have double-sewn thumbs with extra thick material at wear points.

POND GLOVES

If you have a skin problem or a cut that hasn't healed, never plunge your bare hands or arms into a pond as you run the risk of infection. Indeed, there is a big risk of wounds or broken skin admitting a waterborne bacterium such as Weil's disease, which is carried by rats. The answer, if you have damaged skin and need to split or plant waterlilies or pondside plants, remove fish or repair a damaged liner, is to wear protective tough, lined PVC gauntlet gloves. They extend to the shoulder and have an elasticated hem.

HOUSE-PLANT MITTS

Keeping large-leaved philodendrons, Swiss cheese plants and crotons glossy and free from dust can be a time-consuming task if you wipe them with a cloth coated with a proprietary leaf-shine chemical. Instead, you can do the job more quickly and easily by wearing a fleecy mitt. Simply caress leaves to remove dust and unclog pores.

LEATHER GLOVES

Durable and a good investment, most brands are constructed from four pieces: palm, fingers, front and back. The best, however, have a seamless palm. Leather is excellent for rough work, such as pruning, sawing and handling prickly shoots; the toughest are double- or treble-stitched. The palm should have two layers of thornproof cowhide, and seams must be on the outside to avoid them blistering your fingers.

When trying on leather gloves, flex your hands to check them for comfort. They must feel smooth. If there's a rough patch, look for a better pair. When leather gloves get wet, dry them slowly in a cool place. Never dry them them on a radiator, as they will stiffen and become uncomfortable to wear.

Cowhide gloves are a good choice as they have a tight and fetching grain. In tests to check their resistance to abrasion, cowhide was about a third more durable than deerskin or goatskin.

Pigskin is also called washable leather. It is just as supple as cowhide and tougher, but less attractive.

For hardworking hands

Waterproof gloves are useful for repotting and when working in damp conditions (left); thornproof gloves are helpful when pruning roses (centre); durable, all-purpose gloves with a long protective cuff are ideal for heavy pruning, digging and building work.

Goatskin and deerskin are a joy to wear but less durable than cow or pigskin, so keep these gloves away from roses and other prickly plants.

Sheepskin is a creamy white and softer to wear but more easily damaged than other hides. Gloves made from it impart an elegant touch when you're using them to lightly tidy borders. The lanolin they secrete keeps hands soft.

MODERN FABRICS

If you suffer from cold hands and your gloves take a long time to warm up, try hide gloves lined with the modern fabric Thinsulate. Its microfibres have a much larger surface area than most other insulating materials so they trap air efficiently to keep fingers warm.

Not only leather but but hard-wearing cotton canvas coated with Nitrile or heavy-duty crinkle latex will safeguard you from thorns and other sharp objects. They will also keep you dry. Choose a pair that snuggly grips your wrists to keep out dirt.

If you're making a new garden, refurbishing a bed or border and need to shift soil, stones, wood and other rough objects, you'll want heavy-duty, abrasion-resistant gloves. Ideal are durable suede gauntlets with extended safety cuffs. The palm side of the middle two fingers should be a separate piece, reinforced with a welt at the seam to improve wear.

Another glove that is strong, thornproof and easy to work with has a heavy-duty cotton back, which makes it flexible, and a palm of Kevlar, found in flak jackets. An elasticated cuff keeps hands clean.

If it's keeping dry in wet conditions that concerns you, but you also want a warm, comfortable and flexible glove that allows you to tackle fiddly jobs, opt for cotton, jersey or canvas.

Coated with a water-resistant substance, its lint-soft interior makes it a pleasure to wear. Most useful are those with a 'gripping' palm.

HEAD AND FACE

You will need two hats: one to protect you from sunlight; the other to keep you dry. Guard against the harmful effects of ultra-violet light with a wide-rimmed and ventilated, white cotton hat, or one made from straw. If you prefer cotton, choose a non-crushable version that you can fold into a bag or pocket until you need it. Try a light, waxed, cotton hat, with or without a peak, for deflecting rain.

If it's cold and dry, keep your head warm with a deerstalker or conventional cap made from wool tweed or mixed-fibre tweed. Warmer still is a fleece cap with earmuffs.

SAFEGUARDING YOUR EYES AND EARS

Using power equipment can be extremely noisy work, and, if cutting or shredding, can throw up splinters and debris that could damage your eyes. It is essential, therefore, to wear the correct protective garb.

Ear protection Earplugs are effective against noise damage from most garden equipment, including mowers, but if you regularly use very loud power tools, seek out proper ear defenders, which fit snugly over the ears and offer a greater degree of protection.

Eye protection Plastic goggles are relatively inexpensive and generally wrap around the side of the head to shield the whole eye area. Try them out, if possible, before you buy, to ensure that they fit properly, particularly if you wear glasses.

Proper headwear

It is sensible to don a hard hat (top) when pruning overhead branches or working at a height; goggles (centre) will protect your eyes from flying foreign objects; keep your ears safe by wearing ear defenders when using noisy power tools (bottom).

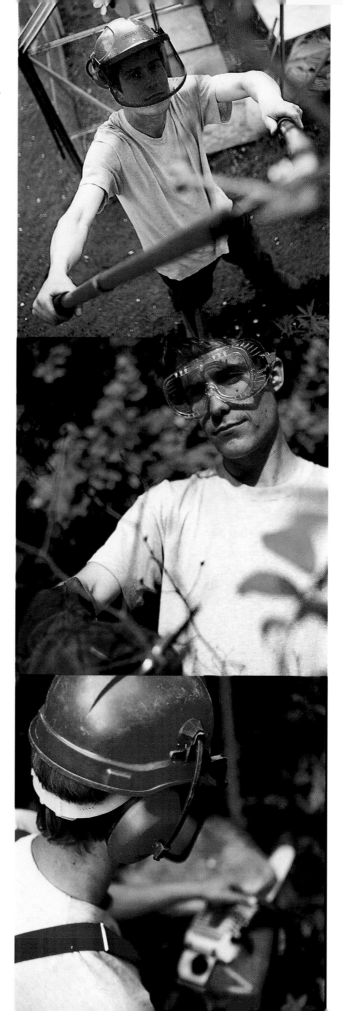

Safeguards & precautions

Certain garden tasks – such as mowing the lawn, trimming the hedge and harvesting fruit from tall trees – entail obvious risks. But even some of the most innocuous-sounding of chores, like hand weeding, are not without their hazards (insect bites, cuts and bruises, rashes, and allergies).

A FAMILY GARDEN

Children and pets can be curious and may not have a sense of danger, so it is sensible to take the following precautions; lock away all chemicals; keep children well away from all lawn equipment when you are using it; make ponds safe by covering them with stout grids; and hang up tools such as spades and forks so children cannot dislodge them.

Ponds and pools are very appealing to children, who love to watch reflections in the surface of the water or try to spot fish swimming about. But you should always be ultra-vigilant if the water is not fenced off or covered with a childproof grid. Such a grid, fixed to rigid beams firmly secured to the pond side, is almost invisible and easily installed. Plants grow well beneath and around it and you can still enjoy the fish.

When the family is enjoying fine weather outside, don't forget to apply sufficient sunscreen, and you may also need insect repellent. Allergies are another common problem, particularly hay fever, so keep an eye on the pollen count if anyone in your family is prone to this.

Younger children love to dig about in the garden. Ensure there are no poisonous plants within their grasp and that they don't put soil-covered hands in their mouths. Also cover sandpits when not in use so they are not soiled by neighbourhood cats.

Install an adequate lock on your garden shed, so children can't stray inside unattended. It is also a good idea to keep your garden generally clutter-free, which will help to prevent accidents.

Climbing the ladder

Never stretch out too far when standing on a ladder as this could cause you or the ladder to topple over. If you have a large area to tackle, keep moving the ladder so that you can easily reach the required spot.

Barbecues are favourites with all the family, but be on guard: position it away from hedges, sheds, fences and overhanging branches, and keep younger children well away from the flames.

USING LADDERS SAFELY

Always position your ladder on a hard, flat surface – never on soft, bumpy or sloping ground. If you are using a power tool or hedging shears on the ladder, don't overreach, as this could cause you to fall. Generally speaking, if you are standing on a platform higher than about 2 metres with a hedge trimmer in your hand, you should have guard rails around you.

Make sure the ladder is tall enough for the job you want to do, as most accidents occur when ladders are too short. Keep your weight evenly distributed while climbing and working on the ladder. Avoid carrying stable. A stepladder version, which can straddle or stand in flower or shrub borders, has large, flat feet to stop it from sinking into the ground. It also has a non-slip platform with generous guard rails which allow you to lean forwards from the platform and safely cut the top of the hedge.

WORKING WITH ELECTRICITY

Statistics reveal that the commonest cause of garden electrical accidents is faulty electric lawn mowers, closely followed by hedge trimmers and lawn trimmers. The simple way to protect yourself from danger is to use a residual current device (RCD). This will automatically monitor the circuit and stop the current from reaching you if you pick up a frayed or severed power cable, or if the machine's electrical insulation is damaged. Fit it to the tool or insert it between the plug and socket: when it senses a fault it

equipment when you climb up. When you reach the top, with your weight balanced, ask someone to pass you the tool you need or take it from your belt.

One of the safest ways to cut a high hedge on uneven or sloping ground is to work from a steel platform with drop legs adjusted to make it level and

Electrical safety

Always check power tools, including plugs and extension leads, before you use them outside, and make sure you have enough flex to allow full mobility.

No hover bother

It's easy, when swinging a hover mower from side to side, to run over and accidentally sever the power cable. This won't happen if you fit snap-tight rotating bright yellow balls, a short distance apart, to the cable. When the machine touches a ball, with the electric cable inside it, it will roll harmlessly out of the way.

<u>Breathe easy</u>

Wear a mask when carrying out dusty work such as shredding. Some brands contain cartridges that filter out chemicals as well, which is useful when spraying.

will cut off power, but it must be reset when a fault has caused it to trip. Other ways to reduce electrical risks are to:

- Keep trailing leads as short as possible and well away from moving blades.
- Get a qualified electrician to install outdoor waterproof sockets.
- Make sure an extension lead is grounded.
- Never use electric tools when it is raining.
- Always disconnect a mower or trimmer from the power supply before examining the blades.

WORKING WITH CHEMICALS

Always read the labels on any product before you use it and follow the recommended instructions precisely. Even organic products can irritate the skin or breathing passages, or damage the eyes if splashing occurs. Never spray when it is windy. Remember to wear long trousers, sleeves and gloves when handling chemicals, and wash your hands thoroughly when you're finished. You should also thoroughly rinse your boots. Finally, many products are poisonous, so keep them well out of the reach of your children.

PROTECT YOUR SPINE

Whether you are reaching for inaccessible areas, hauling unwieldy equipment or moving heavy containers, always take steps to safeguard your spine. Always bend your knees when shifting cumbersome objects, rather than trying to support all the weight from your back. And try to keep a straight spine when digging, too. If you're troubled by back problems, look into acquiring a back support.

CHAIN SAW WISDOM

A chain saw is a quick and efficient tool for removing small and large tree limbs and sawing up logs. If you have use of one, but have never been trained in its use, ask an expert to teach you how to use it safely.

　　You must also wear protective clothing that can 'breathe' to stop you from getting hot and sweaty. Even if you intend only occasionally to use a chain saw, we recommend the following:

- Helmet with mesh visor and ear defenders.
- Jacket, ideally with protective blocking material – a matted fibre that clogs the mechanism and stops the machine should the blade of the saw get into the jacket.
- Chain saw mittens with blocking material in the back of the left hand.
- Seatless trousers with all-round blocking material, to be worn over jeans or ordinary trousers.
- Gaiters, with blocking material.
- Steel toe-capped boots.

8

Gardening with Ease

Specialized tools

Gardening can be very physically demanding and the enjoyable exertions of a morning mowing grass, raking moss and pulling weeds deserve the reward of a long, hot bath followed by a cool drink of iced tea. But if you find the mower unreasonably heavy after a few minutes' work or your back aches after a little light weeding then you should refine your tools to take the strain.

Help is at hand from tool manufacturers who have crafted a range of gadgets to help us tackle most jobs with ease, from mowing to hoeing, weeding to digging, and pruning to watering.

You can find implements to save you bending, kneeling and over-exerting your arms and hands, and many tools if you tire easily. Tools have been fashioned for gardeners confined to a wheelchair or with a weak grip, and for those who are visually impaired. If standing upright for any period of time becomes difficult, choose a tool that lets you work from a sitting position, such as long-handled trowels and hand forks, specially designed hoes and cultivators, weed knives with telescopic handles and weeders.

If strength is an issue, remember that the more leverage you have with a tool, the easier it is to operate. Use ratchet pruners and loppers for pruning, and forks, trowels, hoes and weeders fitted with pistol-grip handles. With such a multitude of operating methods, make sure you try all the tools within a section to find those that work best for you.

WEED CONTROL

Weeds are a perennial problem for gardeners and unless you are exceptionally fortunate, you will have to deal with weeds germinating and competing with your cultivated plants for most of the year. If it's hard for you to find the time or energy to weed, you may

Lopping with ease

Cutting high branches or reaching deeper into a plant is made easy with the use of a ratchet lopper. Relax your upper body and arms to use loppers effectively.

Regular weeding with the golf-club hoe
means never having to stoop. Small weeds
will wither on the surface of the soil and
may not need to be collected by hand.

decide to suppress weeds with a mulch of perforated
plastic, pulverized bark, grass cuttings or carpet. You
should clear existing weeds before laying a mulch to
avoid weeds flourishing underneath.

However, if you enjoy weeding – and many
gardeners find it relaxing – you should consider
several well-designed tools to keep intruders at bay.

HOEING WEEDS
Conventional push hoes and draw hoes require some
effort, but not the golf-club hoe which has three
cutting edges for weeding, as well as taking out seed
drills and earthing up potatoes. Its lightweight,
aluminium alloy shaft has a comfortable contoured
grip, which you hold while you ease the blade back

and forwards through the soil to slice off weeds. The
shape of the head lets you to work comfortably
amongst border perennials and shrubs, and is less
likely to damage plants than an orthodox hoe.

Push-pull weeders have serrated and double-sided
blades that you could use with a push-pull action just
below the soil surface. They are good for weeding in
the vegetable plot or flower borders as they have side
guards to protect nearby plants.

For rogue weeds growing on a patio or between
paving, try a long-armed weeding knife, which you
can use comfortably from a sitting position. It is
essentially a strong steel blade with a hooked end,
designed to prise weeds and moss from between
paving slabs and other cracks.

EXTRACTING WEEDS
Harpoon-like weed extractors are great for removing
those tenacious dandelions, along with other deep-
rooted weeds. Push them into the ground close to the
weed you want to dig up, and then twist and pull to
extract the roots and all.

Weeding while standing
Long-handled flame wands remove the knee
and backache from weeding. Fuelled by
butane or butane and propane gas canisters,
a flame wand is lightweight and easy-to-use.

Another way to extricate weeds without bending (but you'll need two hands) is to arm yourself with a plunger weeder. Simply position its cone of spike-like tines over a weed and push down on the foot plate. Twist gently and extract the weed in an instant. Remove the trapped weed by pressing down on the plunger. You can fill the holes it leaves in a lawn by turning the soil plug and weed upside down and putting them back in the hole.

Similar in function is the weed puller, made from rust-resistant steel with a cadmium-plated blade and claw, and a shaft with a trigger-like grip. Insert the blade beside the weed and loosen the plant by wiggling the tool around. Squeeze the trigger to make the claw grip the weed before levering it out. You can use it single-handed – but you'll need a strong wrist.

SCORCHING WEEDS

If hoeing or pulling up weeds seems like too much effort, why not burn them into oblivion with a flame gun? There are two types of burner: one is an electric gun that blasts air up to around 590°C onto weeds; the other is a small burner connected to a propane gas cylinder. Whichever you use, tackle weeds in two or three bursts. Initially shrivel them – then, a few days later, burn them off. Pernicious weeds sprout from below soil level and need treating several times.

Adapted handles

This bicycle-handled fork protects the wrists from strain while relieving soil compaction. Comfortable grips and a long handle mean you can stand upright while using it.

KNEELING PRETTY

If you cannot bend or crouch, don't risk kneeling directly on the ground to weed. If you do, you may succumb to housemaid's knee – a painful condition caused by pressure or strain in which the fluid-filled sac in front of the kneecap becomes inflamed. Guard against this by using a kneeler stool made from stove-enamelled tubular steel or plastic. It has hand supports to help you get up or down, and a comfortable, soft, knee pad. If you turn it upside down – so that hand supports become legs – you have a seat from which to sow seeds, repot plants or weed.

For greater mobility, strap on a pair of comfortable knee pads. Most are made from water-resistant, stretchy, high-density foam with adjustable fastenings to ensure a snug fit. No matter how wet the ground, you'll stay dry and eager to continue gardening.

DIGGING AND CULTIVATING

You can sprain your wrists from digging in autumn and hoeing in spring, especially if you are unused to these jobs. Both can also damage muscles in your neck, shoulders or back. If you cannot garden as well as once you did, try using specially designed tools that take the strain and help you enjoy being outdoors!

'What a man needs in gardening is a cast-iron back with a hinge in it.'

CHARLES DUDLEY WARNER, WRITER (1829–1900)

SPADES AND FORKS

A new generation of longer, lighter spades and forks encourage a more upright digging stance, which may protect your back from discomfort or injury. Their curved shafts and inward-angled D-handles make digging and forking a confidently safe pleasure.

There are two clever fork variations: one consists of four strong tines on the same plane and an easy-twist bicycle handle with comfortable grips. Use it standing bolt upright for removing weeds or breaking up compacted soil around plants.

The other variation, also used when standing, comprises four, angled tines at the end of a long shaft that are twisted into the soil. This also comes with a bicycle handle. Use both throughout the year for loosening rain-compacted soil around border plants and shrubs, or for breaking up ground before raking to make a seedbed. You can also use it prior to planting out bedding plants and perennials, or for incorporating granular fertilizer or organic mulch. Wipe blades clean with an oily cloth.

CULTIVATORS

If you need to aerate and crumble your soil but have difficulty using a spade or fork, there are several tools that will help you do the job. A long-handled hand fork is great for teasing out weeds and aerating borders without bending too much. Its lightweight head and cranked, tubular shaft make light work of tilling a border.

Pistol-grip tools This family of tools comprises a fork, trowel, weeder, hoe and cultivator. The heads are made of stainless steel to reduce soil adhesion and a heavy-duty plastic handle is attached at right angles to the working head so you can grip the tool firmly in a stress-free position.

If you have weak hands or wrists, lock the tool into an arm-support cuff to harness forearm strength. Some manufacturers produce long-reach versions of the trowel, fork, cultivator and hoe.

Soil crumbler A joy to use either standing up or sitting down, its four sharp, star-wheel tines at the front are connected to a rocking pendulum. In the process of pushing it back and forwards you can pulverize lumpy soil to about 10 cm deep and the blade at the back cuts the heads off weeds. It's heavy to lift – except when resting on the soil – and you can use it one-handed for tilling soil between vegetables or flowers, or for incorporating manure or fertilizer.

Automatic digging

This machine, in vogue a decade ago, allowed gardeners to dig three times faster than their normal rate and with much reduced effort. A foot resting on the rear arm steadied the tool while the arms did most of the work.

Tools on a budget

Tools are likely to be your biggest initial financial investment in gardening – but how do you decide which are vital and which you can do without? Here we outline a basic tool kit for those on a budget.

If you're new to gardening, you are not alone in feeling bewildered by the array of tools available and daunted by the costs involved in kitting yourself out.

One solution, especially if you are furnishing a house at the same time, would be to acquire a set of second-hand tools from family or friends or at car-boot sales.

If you are enthusiastic, however, you may prefer to buy new tools. If you've never gardened before and are unsure whether you will truly take to it, don't buy the best, for it may be abandoned later. If you find yourself wavering, choose sturdy, well-designed and comfortable tools that are relatively cheap. Manufacturers grade their tools from high quality to utility, so there's a good range of standards to choose from. Whatever basic kit of cultivating tools you buy, look for carbon-steel heads. Shafts or handles should be of lightweight polypropylene, steel or wood.

Digging and cultivating
Your first tool should be a digging spade (pages 12–17): use it to turn over ground, make trenches and create planting holes. It should be about 1 metre long and have a D-shaped handle.

Your second most important acquisition will be a digging fork (pages 18–19). Slightly shorter than a spade, but similarly constructed, it's invaluable for forking over and pulverizing heavy ground, crumbling soil for seedbeds, shifting garden compost into a wheelbarrow, aerating a lawn or loosening soil around plants. If you are digging a planting hole and come to a compacted stony layer, you will need a fork to prise out stones. Check that there are no sharp edges or protruding rivets that could blister your hands.

You will need a steel rake if you are preparing seedbeds, sowing flowers or vegetables, or levelling a site for a lawn from seed or turf.

Building a tool kit
A set of tools passed down from a family member or friend can be a wonderful way to begin your own collection (left). Alternatively, buy new tools from a garden centre (above), where you will be able to test the tools for size and comfort before making a purchase.

Buying new tools

Look for a tread – a flattened piece of metal – on top of the blade of a new spade (far left) to make digging more comfortable. A plastic watering can (centre left) is perfectly adequate for new gardeners. Some tools, such as this 'spork' (left), can do more than one job.

stones or roots. For more on hand tools, refer to pages 33–7.

When buying a watering can, choose a sturdy plastic can, which will be far cheaper than metal and equally efficient. A 7-litre model, with capacity indicator lines and a detachable oval brass rose will serve you well. Unless your garden is very small, you will also need a hose. See also pages 42–8.

Cutting and hauling

For pruning, deadheading and trimming, secateurs are the tool of choice. Whether you choose a bypass type or anvil model (pages 68–71), make sure that hardened steel blades are coated with a non-stick substance. Handles, if metal, should be plastic coated.

You won't need a wheelbarrow unless you have a large quantity of soil to shift, or are levelling ground or moving manure. If that's the case, choose a medium-sized, polypropylene barrow with a 45-litre tray, pneumatic wheel and one-piece frame with skids and comfort grips. This will be easier to manoeuvre than a heavily loaded small barrow (pages 104–7).

If you have a lawn, you'll need a mower. This may seem like a big investment, but it will make your life infinitely easier. Choose a model that suits the size and layout of your garden: pages 58–63.

Check that there are 12 well-defined teeth and that the handle is the right length to ensure that you can use it smoothly and rhythmically; see also pages 31–2.

For tackling weeds from early spring to late autumn you can rely on a Dutch hoe (page 30). Also known as a push hoe, it's a tool that beheads weeds, as well as aerating the soil around annuals, border plants and shrubs.

Planting and watering

When it comes to planting, you will need a trowel. This small hand tool is ideal for working in window boxes and containers, as well as in your beds and borders. Or consider a hand fork. Designed for planting bulbs, alpines, spring and summer bedding annuals and herbaceous plants, it should have strong tines that won't flex or bend in heavy or compacted soil, or when you meet

The soil crumbler digs deeper in light, sandy soil than heavy clay. Brush soil from tines if they clog, and lubricate the spindle and pivot points with a spray of oil to keep them moving freely.

Mini cultivator These three-pronged devices are good for keeping small beds and borders tidy. Connect them to three lengths of handle (38 cm, 70 cm and a 86–149 cm telescopic pole) to aerate heavy or light soil between plants or loosen weeds so they shrivel and die. Some models have a weed-cutting blade attached to the tines.

PRUNING AND CUTTING

Pruning can be a tough job if you have weak arms and wrists, particularly when cutting through tough branches and stems. Conventional cutting tools, including anvil or bypass pruners, loppers and saws, are relatively easy to use if you have average arm and wrist strength. But if you haven't, and still wish to prune trees, shrubs, climbers and fruit trees, you should use ratchet cutters, long handles or pulleys to give you greater leverage. Remember to grease pivot points with a lubricating oil to keep the action fluid.

RATCHET ACTION

Sturdy ratchet pruners or secateurs greatly multiply wrist leverage – 30 per cent less pressure is needed – and allow you to cut branches up to 2 cm thick. You can prune thin shoots in one attempt while tackling thicker stems in stages. To operate, grip the stem with the pruners, squeeze the handles until you meet resistance and release pressure until you hear a click. This brings the stepped cutting device into play. Squeeze the handles again and the blade will bite further into the stem. One or two more bites (to a maximum of four) will sever the stem.

Ratchet pruners These are light and strong with handles made from heavy-duty plastic, or nylon and fibreglass. Anvil types have a hardened steel blade, which cuts onto a heavy-duty plastic anvil. In the case of the bypass pruners, a sharpened blade slices alongside an anvil.

Ratchet loppers These work on the same principle as ratchet pruners, in which robust, oval, tubular steel handles are bolted to a blade and anvil. Ratchet loppers allow you to cut 5-cm branches easily in several bites. Use them throughout the year to remove branches from shrubs and trees or cut out thick shoots from the middle of rose bushes. You can replace both the blade and anvil.

CUT-AND-GRIP PRUNERS

These comfortable anvil secateurs weigh as little as 200 grams and are designed to slice through a stem and hold on to it: a big advantage when you're working from a sitting position. They have an easy, single-hand-operated catch, which you can use for gathering flowers or pruning roses and other shrubs.

Another model, which is long-shafted and versatile, has a trigger-grip handle and a 360 degree swivel cutting head. Use it for removing twiggy shoots from climbing roses, woody shrubs, holly and other thorny bushes; and also for deadheading, cutting dead leaves from waterlilies and picking fruit.

COMPRESSED AIR PRUNERS

Operated by a compressor, the double-piston system pneumatic pruner uses seven to ten bars of air pressure to make quick, clean, and most importantly,

Cutting back hard

Hard pruning this spring-flowering shrub is easy with a long-handled pruner. The longer the tool's arms, the greater the leverage it has to cut.

Ratchet pruners are designed for you to cut through tough shoots up to 2 cm wide with ease. Squeeze the handles up to four times to cut through stems without twisting or straining your wrists.

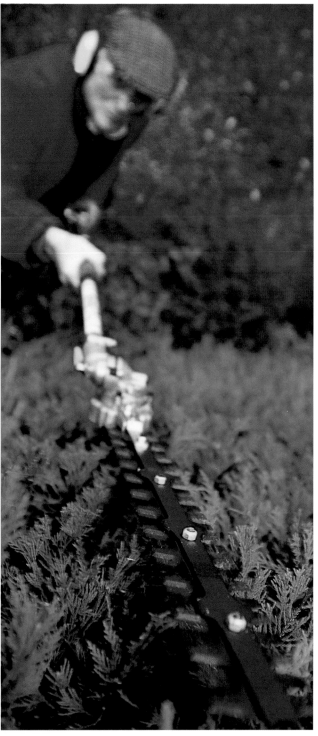

effortless cuts. Use it from spring to autumn for pruning fruit trees and bushes, ornamental shrubs, climbers and roses.

Left hands If you're left-handed and find it awkward to use traditional pruners, you'll be heartened to know that one or two companies make a left-handed pruner. These bypass tools have an appetite for shoots as wide as 18 mm, with a rust-resisting blade opened by an easily flicked catch.

Long-handled pruner If you've just moved house and cannot reach the limbs of inherited trees and shrubs to trim them, do the job using a long-handled pruner with a heavy-duty operating cord. The head is worked by two pulleys that double pruning power. Choose a head that you can lock into a lightweight telescopic pole, extending your reach to as much as 5 metres.

TRIMMING HEDGES

A boundary hedge is an asset: prized for the privacy it provides and the street noise it muffles. But it needs regular shearing to keep it tidy. If you have weak wrists or shoulders – or are not strong enough to use an electric hedge trimmer – use hedging shears.

There are several specially designed hedging shears with extra-long alloy handles to increase leverage,

Within reach

A 2-metre hedge in need of trimming won't be beyond you if you buy lightweight electric hedge trimmers with a telescopic arm.

Lawn tools for less effort

The lawn is one of the toughest parts of the garden to maintain. Ride-on mowers make light work of cutting the grass, as do cordless shears of ragged lawn edges.

which weigh as little as 700 g. Their carbon- or stainless-steel blades are razor sharp and, despite repeated use, remain efficient for a long time before they need sharpening. Some blades are pressed with moulded inserts to increase strength and reduce friction, and stainless-steel blades are replaceable. Use shears with telescopic handles if you need to reach across a wide hedge.

You may want to try gear-handled shears if your hedge is twiggy with thick shoots. These have a branch notch to help cut shoots up to 1 cm wide.

If you've moved to a garden with a high hedge and feel unsafe cutting it from a stepladder, there are extendible shears for the purpose. Essentially, a wavy-edged shear-head slots into a lightweight telescopic pole – head and pole weigh only 900 g and 350 g respectively – and a strong cord operates the levered cutting head. Tug just once on the cord in order to cut a specific stem, and pull it repeatedly if you want to cut continuously. You will need both hands to hold the pole.

LAWN LORE

If you can't bend comfortably, suffer from arthritic joints or experience back pain, you may find it difficult to mow, edge, rake and aerate a lawn with conventional machines and tools. Some manufacturers are now aware of these problems and have designed mowers and other gadgets to meet your needs.

MOWERS

If you're in good health but have little energy, you will probably prefer a lightweight and manoeuvrable lawn mower. You can choose from a range of specially designed cylinder, rotary or hover machines to suit

your budget, power supply and taste in lawn stripes! Some 32-cm cylinder models weigh less than 10 kg with four-blade cylinders and seven height-of-cut adjustments (from 12–42 mm). Full-width rear rollers ensure those coveted green stripes and energy-efficient motors keep the mowers moving.

There are several light rotary mowers with four wheels and a 30-cm blade. Most have large grass boxes, three cutting heights, and weigh 8 kg.

Electric hover mowers are ideal for trimming banks and other uneven areas. They ride on a cushion of air and are usually 'swept' across the lawn. A plastic or metal blade cuts the grass, which is left on the surface or sucked into a grass box. Smaller models weigh just 4.5 kg with an 28-cm plastic blade, and have an adjustable height of cut. Some models are motorized and have a pivotal head to help you steer them.

TRIMMING LAWN EDGES

The handles of heavy, long-handled edging shears are often too short and, in bending awkwardly, the job becomes arduous and straining. The comfortable

'If only one were as good a gardener in practice as one is in theory, what a garden one would create'

VITA SACKVILLE-WEST, WRITER AND GARDENER (1892–1962)

answer is to use a single-shafted model rather than a conventional two-handled model. Swivel its blades into a vertical or horizontal position to cut edges or flat areas around paths, seats and other objects.

Single-handed shears are for people who are not able to stand to manage a long-handled shear. With these you can kneel or sit – the easy, effortless, lightweight answer is a single-handed swivel shear. It cuts grass cleanly with spring-loaded, steel blades operated by a trigger-action lever. Rotate the blades – not your arm – through 180 degrees to neaten the sides of a lawn or flat areas that the mower can't reach. You can also use these shears for trimming topiary that is made from box, yew or privet, as well as for removing soft shoots from alpines, heathers and other shrubs.

Cordless shears are easier to use for cutting flat strips of lawn adjoining walls, fences and garden sculpture. They are light with a robust motor and have easily sharpened, hardened steel blades, which are specially coated in order to prevent them from rusting and accumulating dirt. You will, of course, have to kneel down to operate the shears. If you find that position awkward, try attaching a single-shaft guide-handle fitted with a safety switch.

Another satisfying and relatively effortless way to level grass around obstacles is to use a lightweight, electric nylon-line trimmer while standing upright. There is little or no pressure exerted on the back muscles and you can use it one- or two-handed. Some models have a variable, swing-easy and wrist-supporting handle, which is designed to avoid fatigue while you trim at full reach.

You can rotate the handle of many models through 180 degrees for cutting lawn edges. If you are taller than average, fit a 15-cm telescopic handle extension to make trimming more comfortable.

RAKING MOSS FROM LAWNS
Removing moss and thatch from grass is no fun if you have a bad back, a slipped disc or muscular problem. Even to attempt raking may seriously aggravate the

problem. But by using an electric scarifier you can keep a lawn aerated (free from clogging, dead grass) and in glowing, good health. This labour-saving ally has a jawful of hooked, steel teeth, a front roller with depth adjuster and a grass box, which comes with a compactor to double capacity and halve trips to the compost bin. (You can even save the moss you collect to line hanging baskets.) With the scarifier's teeth set high you can also pick up leaves to make leaf mould.

AERATING COMPACTED TURF
Periodically, especially in the autumn, you should spike the lawn and compacted patches of heavy soil to let in air and revitalize root growth. If you are fit, you can do this with a garden fork, stabbing the grass to the full depth of the fork's tines at 15-cm intervals. Then use the back of a steel rake to work into the holes an equal parts mix of sharp sand and topsoil.

Multi-functional barrow
If a single-wheeled barrow is difficult to balance, try a lightweight cart of UV-treated resin with two wheels and a stabilizer.

An easier method for those with slightly less energy is to use a hollow-tine aerator to create drainage holes up to 6 cm deep. Operate this by pressing your foot on to the aerator's platform to eject plugs of soil from tines at either end.

If using a hollow-tined device makes you breathless, strap a pair of spiked soles to your boots and walk slowly over the grass. The holes you make will help your lawn breathe more easily and allow water to percolate into it – and you may enjoy the exercise.

CARRYING WATER

The old-fashioned yoke our ancestors used showed how aware they were of the importance of distributing a load evenly when lifting and carrying. If you want to keep your back and spine in good shape, particularly while watering, it may not be very wise to use a round, metal watering can. In holding it away from your legs to stop it from bruising them, it's easy to strain your back, arm and wrist muscles. A rectangular plastic watering can, which holds around 5 litres is a far better choice for your back, or else you could use two smaller cans and carry one in each hand to balance the load.

WATERING WITHOUT A HOSE REEL

If bending causes you pain, forget about unwinding and rewinding a hose reel. Instead, irrigate beds and borders with a porous pipe zig-zagged through them that has been buried 3 cm or so beneath the surface of the soil. When you want to water, all you have to do is connect a short length of hose from the outside tap or water butt to the near end of the porous pipe that you have left protruding from the soil. Water feeds through the hose and onto the soil. Use it to water shrubs, flower beds and borders, window boxes, lawns, roses, vegetables, narrow flower beds alongside paths, hedges and fruit trees.

This trick works best with water at low pressure, so open the tap by only a quarter to half a turn to irrigate about 1 metre of soil either side of the hose.

Watering wisely

Avoid round watering cans to protect your back, as holding full cans away from your body can cause strain. Opt instead for flat-sided plastic cans. Choose a handle that helps to tilt the can so that you do not twist your arm or shoulder as you water.

Computerized watering

Water can be transported from tap to flowerbed through an automated watering system. The hose, which can sometimes be buried under the surface of the soil, is pumped with water at pre-set times and quantities. This system is also helpful if you are often away from home.

Accessories to help you water the entire garden include straight, tee and elbow connectors, in-line taps, water filters, pressure reducers and a double-check valve to prevent risk of water 'back-siphoning' and contaminating your source.

HANGING BASKET WATERER

Choose hanging baskets that can be lowered when you need to water or opt for one of the following easy options. Connect a hose to a lightweight spray wand. Choose a model that extends from around 75 to 120 cm. It should also have finger-tip on-off control and come with a spray head that delivers ultra-fine droplets for penetrating deep into the compost.

Alternatively, automate watering by installing a computer-regulated, drip-feed system. With this you can spray, mist or drizzle plants, or accurately drip water into the soil to ensure it is moist at all times. The heart of the system is an electronic water timer that you can set to deliver a certain volume of water up to several times a day.

SETTING YOUR SIGHTS

If you enjoy the great outdoors, an inability to see clearly needn't spoil the pleasures that gardening brings you. With a little practice in orientation – aided by paths of varying textures, hand rails, focal points at a set distance apart, wind chimes, scented or bright shrubs – you will soon discover how easy it is to locate key areas.

Of course, there are problems, but it's very satisfying when you resolve them. For example, it's vital to cover the tops of canes and other thin plant supports with rubber or cork toppers to make them safe.

FINDING TOOLS

A big problem in not being able to see clearly is that when you put down a tool, you are inclined to lose it. So, after using a trowel, hand hoe, pruners or other small tool – which should be vivid red or another bright colour – don't put it on the ground, return it to a tool-belt holder.

Holders come in several shapes and sizes. Among them are three- and four-pocket tool pouches, three-pocket bib aprons, and two-pocket waist aprons. Most are made from durable, lightweight nylon with mesh pockets that allow soil to filter out. Edges and straps are often made of nylon webbing and stress points are reinforced with rivets.

Buckets are excellent for holding hand tools and their usefulness is greatly increased if you strap a 'holdall' around one. You'll be amazed at what you can transport around the garden that will save you walking to and from the house and shed.

A green hose reel can be invisible on a lawn – and it could trip you up. Why not use a bright yellow one instead? In winter, its colour may even cheer you up!

Keeping in sight

If your eyesight is reduced, ensure your tools are highly visible. Return hand tools to your tool belt until you next need them (above). Green-coloured tools and hoses that blend in with the lawn can become obstacles to trip over; instead, seek out tools with bright colours that you won't miss (right).

9

Looking after Your Tools

Safeguarding your tools

When you find a tool that works for you – whether it's a hoe, daisy grubber or cuttings knife – hang onto and protect it with a passion. If you lose or break it, you may never find another like it. Good gardening tools are your friends – they work with you to achieve reliable results with comfort and ease. Chosen carefully, after much deliberation, you want them to endure, and the longer you have them, the more you cherish them. They may require little more than a rub with an oily cloth to protect them from rust, decay and the eventual need to replace them. But it's knowing when to apply that oily cloth that can save you substantial time, expense and anxiety.

WASHING DIRTY TOOLS

Never put away used spades, forks, hoes, cultivators and steel rakes without cleaning them first. This is particularly important if you garden on clay soil which coats tools with a hard, dry crust. Initially, wash them with the garden hose. If you can't hose them down – handles and all – use a bucket of water and a

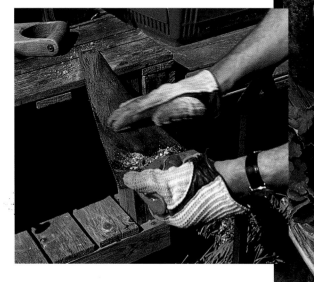

The value of maintenance
Neglected metal tools will languish; rub them with oily sand to remove patches of rust (above). When well oiled and cared for, your tools will last you a lifetime (right).

scrubbing brush. If they are only slightly soiled with mud, you can use a wooden or plastic scraper to remove it.

When metal blades and handles are clean and dry, wipe them with an oily cloth or spray them with a petroleum-based lubricant and rust inhibitor. Alternatively, plunge spades and forks several times into a bucket of oily sand before storing them. Preserve wooden handles by wiping them with a cloth soaked in linseed oil.

PROTECTING YOUR KNIFE

A clean, sharp knife is vital for making cuts that will heal quickly when you propagate your plants by budding, grafting, layering or taking cuttings. Wipe any sticky plant sap from the blade with a solvent based on mineral spirits, and follow this by rubbing the blades with an oiled cloth. Sap left on blades will usually turn black and make further cutting difficult. If the sap has been left to harden, remove it with an emery cloth or wire brush attached to a power drill.

When not in use, keep all cutting tools in a dry, cool place (out of the reach of children) where moisture won't attack and rust blades. After cleaning blades and other metal parts, coat them with a rust-inhibiting lubricant and squirt thin oil where blades pivot to keep them moving freely. Coat wooden handles with linseed oil.

MAINTAINING MOWERS

Whichever lawn mower you have, its efficiency will be determined by the maintenance you give it. A cursory wipe of the blades will not be good enough after the

---

SPRING CLEANING YOUR MOWER

Carry out all cleaning jobs on a firm, paved or concrete surface. Use a stiff brush to remove caked-on grass and soil from blades, grass-collection box and rollers. If you have a rotary or hover mower, remove mud from under the canopy. The best tool for this is a stout plastic or wooden scraper. Follow by massaging all metal areas with a rag soaked in thin oil and lubricate the chain and other moving parts. Rest the machine on a thick layer of newspapers to catch mud, grass clippings and drops of oil. Store in a dry, airy shed or garage.

---

muddy business of cutting a lawn. If you want your machine to serve you well, you must spend more than a few minutes cleaning and checking it.

Electric machines Do not attempt to clean an electric mower until you have unplugged the machine and disconnected the power supply. Then remove mud and grass clippings with a stiff brush and oil the machine's moving parts. Check cables for cuts. If you find one or more, repair it with a waterproof connector or, ideally, replace the cable.

When the cutting season ends, examine leads for loose connections and tighten if necessary. If cables are worn or inner plastic-coated wires are visible – no matter how slightly – repair them with waterproof connectors or replace altogether.

Petrol mowers Before cleaning your petrol-powered machine in the manufacturer's recommended way, use up the fuel in the carburettor to prevent it from going stale by leaving the engine running with the drive disengaged and the fuel tap shut off. The engine will cut out once it has used the fuel in the carburettor.

Check the oil level too. If the oil is black, it is time to change it. If you find yourself frequently topping up the sump, check for leaks, as oil dripping on to your

For extra security

When not in use, keep your knives and other cutting implements in a holster. This will not only help to keep the blades sharp, but will also protect you from accidental cuts.

grass will kill it. Periodically examine the air filter with a view to cleaning it if it's dirty or changing it if it's become damaged.

When the cutting season ends, put your petrol-powered mower to bed properly. Drain off all fuel to avoid leaving any in the cylinder and replace the engine oil with a fresh supply. Clean the spark plug with a wire brush and set the gap to comply with that recommended in the manufacturer's handbook.

Battery-powered mowers After cleaning the machine, immediately recharge the battery. Every two weeks, check the level of distilled water in the battery cells and, if necessary, top it up. Use a rag to clean dirt from battery terminals. If dry, smear them with petroleum jelly.

When the cutting season ends, remove and clean the battery and top up cells with fresh distilled water. Recharge the battery and store it in a warm, dry place, ideally on a wooden base, to keep it above the floor.

Rotary and hover mowers The blade of a rotary or hover mower may be a long strip of metal with two cutting edges, or a triangular blade that you remove from a rotating, circular, metal disc. Either should be sharpened by securely clamping them into a vice and taking a flat file to them.

Take care, when sharpening strip blades, to remove the same amount of metal from each end. It's vital that the blade remains level when you have sharpened it. Test the blade for balance by suspending it on a nail or screwdriver: if one end points up, sharpen the other end until the metal bar is horizontal.

A stitch in time...

Spray lubricating oil onto metal joints to stop them from becoming stiff (left). Always remove any grass cuttings trapped under the blade of the mower so they don't clog the machine (centre). Use a rag soaked in linseed oil to keep wooden handles smooth and stop them them from cracking.

Cylinder mowers Unlike rotary and hover mowers which cut by slashing grass, a cylinder blade rotates against a fixed bottom blade and cuts with a scissor action. Refine the cylinder by attaching a sharpening strip to the bottom blade and adjusting the cylinder so that it lightly brushes against it. If you are unsure, you can have the cylinder sharpened professionally.

Curing rust Remove any rust by rubbing it with emery paper or a wire brush. Restore treated areas by painting them with red oxide and follow this with an undercoat and gloss top coat.

SHARPENING YOUR TOOLS

All cutting tools must be sharp. If not, they are hard to use and leave ragged cuts on your plants that may become diseased. Blunt knives can also be dangerous, for they tend to slip away from a shoot rather than cut into it properly.

The sharper your secateurs and loppers, the cleaner their cuts will be and the more quickly they will heal. Unless pruning saws are sharp, with correctly set teeth, they will bind, especially in sappy wood.

> **'He that would perfect his work must first sharpen his tools.'**
> CONFUCIUS, PHILOSOPHER (551–479 BC)

You should always keep spade and hoe blades sharp. Blunted tools take longer and more effort to slice through the soil.

Sharpening equipment To sharpen your knives, secateurs, loppers, scythes, sickles, axes and shears you will need a medium-fine flat file – some brands are impregnated with diamond particles. Alternatively, to produce a razor-sharp edge invest in a grinding stone. Choose from coarse or fine grades of synthetic or natural grinding stones. Whichever you use, moisten it with water, oil or petrol before use; its instructions will tell you which lubricant to use when you buy it. Otherwise you won't build up a paste of stone particles, vital for honing a blade, and the stone will quickly wear out.

Hand sharpening If practicable, dismantle your secateurs, loppers and hand- and long-handled shears to sharpen them more easily, setting the blade in a vice. You can sharpen a blade more accurately this way than by holding it in your hand. Remember, if you are using a file, hold the tip in one hand and the handle in the other, and lightly press it against the blade. Push it away from you. Remove it from the blade when you've finished a stroke... and start again. A file is not designed to be used backwards.

If hand sharpening takes too long or is physically demanding, tighten the blade in a vice and create a keen, new edge in seconds by using a grinding stone connected to an electric drill. Sparks will fly, so wear safety goggles and gloves.

After sharpening all blades, coat them with water-repelling oil – especially if the air is damp – to stop rust attacking them and impairing their efficiency.

Chain saws These require precise sharpening with a round file or they won't cut well. If your hands are unsteady or you find it difficult to file at the correct angle, use a precision filing tool mounted securely on a work bench.

Hedge trimmers Brush the blades of electric hedge trimmers with mineral spirit to remove clogging prunings and sticky sap before wiping them clean and spraying them with an anti-rust lubricant. Examine the cable for abrasions and repair it with a waterproof connector, or replace altogether.

STORING YOUR TOOLS

Never store garden tools in a random heap. It's not easy to find the one you want and searching for it is exasperating and dangerous. In discovering hand shears and other small hand tools tucked away behind larger ones, a carelessly positioned spade, fork, rake, hoe or saw may fall upon you. Helpful guidelines when storing tools include:

- Don't hang your tools too high. It's physically demanding to position them well above ground, and also hazardous! You could be impaled by a garden fork that slips from your fingers.
- Tools, no matter what shape or weight, should remain where you put them.
- Position them so that handles or working heads are just above floor level.

Guidelines for sharpening

Be careful, when you are using either a file (far left) or a sharpening stone (left), to draw it across the blade, from tip to heel, at the same angle at which the blade was sharpened when it left the factory.

Handy hooks

Secure a tool rack on one wall of your shed so that you can suspend light implements off the floor and out of harm's way (left). Bulky equipment should be hung from large, securely fixed hooks (above).

Storing methods The easiest way of storing tools is to screw strong and generous hooks onto a stout wooden backboard secured to the wall of your shed or garage. Alternatively, use dowels, angled slightly upwards and securely glued into place. Yet another way is to fix a peg board to the wall and hang tools from hooks locked into it. Nails and screws must be long enough and their heads large enough to ensure that tools cannot be dislodged if you brush against them. Check regularly that the nails have not loosened.

If you use snap-in steel grippers – some kinds glide on a track for random spacing – do not overload them with tools heavier than they are designed to support. Large, heavy-duty hooks are useful on their own for storing bulky tools or linked to take ladders and wheelbarrows.

Tool bags Hung on a shed, garage or greenhouse wall, a simple pocketed strip of hessian about 100 x 30 cm in size, with a handle, makes a perfect home for small tools. Here you can store your hand forks, trowels, cultivators, secateurs, knives, sheep shears and widgers which, when you've finished with them, are easily misplaced. If your tool kit consists of a selection of interchangeable working heads that slot into a common short, intermediate, long or telescopic handle, then storing heads and handles is easy with a purpose-made support rack. Screwed vertically to a wall, it comes with sturdy upwards-facing sockets for tool heads. There are handle holders too.

SHEDS AND TOOL STORES

A shed should be cool and airy in summer, warm and dry in winter, with light flooding through generous windows. Home to a mix of assorted implements, it should also be well-organized. You must know where a particular tool is and be able to find it quickly.

Size and siting The larger a shed, within reason, the easier it is to store tools – many of which you haven't yet bought! So think of a size, then double it.

In addition to garden tools, you may want a work bench and power equipment and space for bicycles. Shelves will help maximize your floor space. A shed must be in perspective with your beds and borders. It

'The man who has planted a garden feels that he has done something for the good of the whole world.'

CHARLES DUDLEY WARNER, WRITER (1829–1900)

must not overshadow your neighbour's garden. It should be as close as practicable to the house, because if you tuck it away at the end of a garden, you will be less inclined to use it in poor weather.

If your garden just isn't large enough for a shed, protect a wide range of tools from weather and theft in a storage chest of selected pine waterproofed with an acrylic-based primer. The lid (roof) should be mineral felted and come with profiled sills to keep out rain.

TYPES OF SHED

There are three basic structures: apex-roofed, pent-roofed and dual-purpose. The big advantage of an apex shed is that its pitched roof, with a central ridge, allows you to build a generous loft for storing long, bulky or rarely used items.

A pent-roofed shed, which is normally set close to a wall or fence has a flat top that gently slopes backwards. Though it lacks the visual appeal of a pitched-roof structure, it is less expensive.

The dual-purpose shed – a practical hybrid combining the assets of a pent-roofed design and a greenhouse – is a good compromise if you haven't room for two structures but enjoy propagating plants.

DO YOU TAKE YOUR TOOLS FOR GRANTED?

- Have you 'mislaid' a favourite garden tool recently?
- When was the last time you cleaned your lawn mower or changed its oil?
- Do you regularly give cleaned knives, secateurs, loppers and other such equipment a rub with an oily rag to protect them from rust?
- When idle, are your tools stored out of harm's way?

If the answer to any of these is yes, then ten minutes at the end of each gardening session can save you money, time and effort that would be better spent on gardening!

Wooden sheds Heat-retaining and sympathetic with plants, softwood (deal) and more expensive western red cedar are traditional and very popular. If you opt for softwood, ensure that it is pressure-treated with preservative to inhibit decay. After assembling the shed, coat it annually with preservative. Usefully, western red cedar is rot-resistant and doesn't need preserving. But its glowing reddish-brown wood will turn a silvery hue if you don't paint it once a year with a cedar stain.

Concrete A robust, concrete shed is best positioned close to the house – rather than in the middle or back of the garden – where its hard lines are incompatible with beds, borders and lawns. Soften walls, usually of exposed aggregate or imitation brick, by coating them with a weather-resistant paint and climbing plants.

Metal It's not the first material you might think of when buying a shed, but models constructed from hot-dipped, galvanized steel, finished with baked-on paint are remarkably handsome. They are robust, with large sliding doors, and have a long and useful life. There are apex and ridge models to choose from.

Though walls are usually window-less, most models have translucent roof panels to ensure that plenty of light illuminates your tools and work bench.

Glossary

Aerate Digging or forking compacted soil to help air percolate down to warm it and to improve root growth.

Anemometer A three-cupped instrument that pivots on a vertical spindle to record the speed of the wind.

Aneroid A portable barometer that can measure atmospheric pressure without the use of any fluid.

Apex roof Found in sheds and other buildings, this is a pitched roof with a central ridge that works to give you extra attic storage space.

Barometer An instrument that measures atmospheric pressure and records changes in weather or altitude.

Besom A broom that is made by tying a bundle of birch or heather twigs to the end of a pole with wire. Use it for sweeping up bulky areas of rubbish.

Biodegradable Material that decomposes into simple elements when attacked by bacteria and other biological processes.

Capillary matting Highly water-absorbent synthetic fibre on which pots are firmly placed. Moisture is drawn from this fibre up into the compost.

Cloche A temporary glass or plastic structure that is placed over outdoor plants to hasten and protect their growth, or to warm the soil before sowing or planting.

Clute-cut glove A glove designed so that the palm is made from one seamless piece of material. This ensures that the wearer's hands have a roomy, comfortable fit.

Compost activator A nitrogen-based substance like manure, fertilizer or comfrey leaves but with additional enzymes and fungi, which are used to accelerate the decomposition of organic waste into fertile, crumbly and nutrient-rich humus.

Deadhead Cut or pinch off the faded blooms of bedding plants, roses and border perennials to ensure that they channel all of their energy into producing more shoots and flowers, rather than unwanted seeds.

Dibber A short, cone-shaped tool, which often has a metal end, handy for making holes in the soil or compost, for inserting cuttings or for planting seedlings, young leeks and brassicas.

Double digging A method of turning over the soil in which a wide trench is taken out and the soil is then dug to a depth of two spits (each a spade blade deep).

Enzymes A group of complex proteins that are produced by living cells and that trigger biochemical reactions. Some compost activators contain enzymes.

Fulcrum The point of support, or pivot, of a lever. A good example is the wheel spindle of a barrow.

Galvanized Steel or iron coated with a layer of rust-proof zinc.

Gore-Tex Durably waterproof but still breathable fabric. Each square centimetre has an amazing four billion holes, which keep rain out but also allow the water vapour from perspiration to escape.

Hormone-rooting powder/liquid A synthetic plant hormone – such as naphthyl acetic acid or indole butyric acid – that stimulates root development. Dip your cuttings into it before inserting them into rooting compost.

Hygrometer An instrument used to measure humidity levels.

Lacewing chamber A wooden box that is designed to attract and provide over-winter protection for beneficial insects called lacewings, which feed on greenfly and many other sucking pests.

Leaf mould Crumbly, blackish-brown material formed by decomposing a heap of leaves. Add it to seed and potting compost or use it as a soil-conditioning mulch.

Microbe A bacterium – either beneficial or harmful – that can only be seen with the aid of a microscope.

Microclimate A small area in which the atmospheric conditions affecting organisms differ from the general climate of the surroundings.

Needle bearings Small, roller-shaped, anti-friction bearings which are situated in the wheel of a barrow and help it to run smoothly.

Neoprene A form of synthetic rubber that is resistant to oil and ageing, and is often used to waterproof clothing.

Non-return valve Fitted between the hose and the mains water source, this valve prevents back-siphoning. It's a good idea to invest in one if you are using a liquid fertilizer, as it prevents contamination of the water supply.

Oasis Also called floral foam, oasis is a cellular plastic material. The green version, when it is used wet, can soak up almost 30 times its volume of water. The brown or grey form tends to be used dry, for dried or artificial flower arrangements.

Oscillating hoe For removing weeds and loosening compacted soil, this has a push-pull, square-shaped rocking head.

Pent roof This is a term that is usually applied to a shed whose roof slopes gently backwards.

Permanent wilting point This is the point when a lack of moisture in the soil forces a plant to use up so much fluid from its own cells that it dies.

Pheromone trap Usually used to control the codling moth, this is a sticky device that is impregnated with the scent of a female moth and then hung in fruit trees to lure and kill male moths.

Pneumatic Containing compressed air. A pneumatic wheelbarrow tyre, for example, which ensures a smooth ride.

Polartec A breathable fleece fabric often used for base and middle layers of outdoor clothing. Sweat is wicked away from the garment to leave skin feeling dry.

Polypropylenes A family of tough, flexible synthetic thermoplastic materials, which are made by polymerizing propylene.

Pricking out Transferring crowded seedlings from a pot or a tray to where they will have more room to grow.

Residual current device An adapter that protects you from being electrified. It works by detecting an earth fault and then cutting off the power as rapidly as possible. Fit it between your power tool and the mains socket.

Saddle joint This joint is one way of fixing a spade head to its handle. Two straps come up from the head, lie flat against the front and back of the handle and are secured with rivets.

Scarification A method of improving growth by using a flexible rake to remove any dead grass and moss from a lawn.

Scion A shoot cut taken from one plant (variety) with the intention of grafting it onto another plant (stock).

Secateurs Anvil type: A straight-edged cutting blade that closes onto a flat bar of metal – often brass – known as the anvil.

Bypass type: Two curved-shape blades brush past one another, cutting with a scissor-like action.

Setting out Planting a tree, shrub, border perennial or any other plant where you want it to grow.

Silica A refractory, insoluble material notably used in the manufacture of glass, ceramics and also abrasives.

Single digging A method of turning over the soil in which only the fertile top layer of soil is dug, and to a depth of only one spit or spade blade.

Socket joint This is a joint that is frequently used in spades. The handle fits into a circular hole at the top of the head and is secured there with rivets that are driven through the shaft.

Spit The depth of a spade blade, usually about 25–30 cm. Soil is usually dug either one or two spits deep.

Sprinkler A watering device that fits on to the end of a hose and sprays droplets over a wide area.

Stamped metal A spade blade that is fashioned from a metal sheet.

Subsoil A zone of usually infertile, poorly textured, and poorly structured soil around 30 cm below the surface.

Tanalize A process of preserving wood in order to keep it rot-free for many years.

Tang-and-ferrule A method of attaching the shaft or handle of a tool to the head, commonly used to make hand tools. The tang is a sharp point on top of the head that fits into the base of the shaft. The ferrule is a metal ring that fits over the joint to hold it closed and to stop the wood from splitting.

Tetanus Also known as lockjaw, this illness is caused by a bacterium found in manure and other organic material. Given the opportunity, it can easily infect injuries, especially those with a deep, dirty and airless puncture wound.

Thinsulate An insulating fabric whose microfibres have a much larger surface area than most alternative materials. It is often used to line gloves.

Tilth A 5–8-cm layer of fine crumbly soil that is produced by raking, and in which to sow seeds.

Tine The prong of a fork, rake or other soil-cultivating implement.

Topsoil The upper 23–30 cm of dark, fertile, humus-rich soil in which plants tend to grow.

Trug A lightweight garden basket that is usually made from sweet chestnut, willow, birch or plaited rush.

Velcro A fastening consisting of two strips of nylon: one having tiny hooked threads; the other a coarse surface into which the threads can mesh.

Weil's disease Another name for leptospirosis, a bacterium that can cause kidney failure, jaundice and meningitis, and is transmitted to humans by rats and other animals. Ponds may also harbour it.

Acknowledgements

Picture researcher Sandra Schneider
Indexer Michele Clarke
IT support Paul Stradling
Production Nigel Reed, Karol Davies

Val Bradley would like to thank the many companies who were so helpful in supplying information, and Steve, Chris and Nick for their patience.

Carroll & Brown would like to thank Pamela and Michael Stewart-Murray, Cornwall for allowing us to photograph in their garden, Paul from Earthworks, and Abdul and Hanis Bharmal at Carpenders Park Nursery.

Picture Credits

t = top; c = centre; b = below; r = right; l = left; GPL = Garden Picture Library

page 2 Ray Main/Mainstream, **6 (tc)** Garden Images, **(cb)** David Murray, **(br)** Plantstuff, **10/11** Ray Main/Mainstream, **12 (b)** Derek St Romaine, **14** David Austin Roses, **17** Derek St Romaine, **18** David Murray, **22** Sneeboer, **25 (c,r)** David Murray, **27** David Murray, **28/29** Jules Selmes, **31** David Murray, **32 (l)** David Murray, **33** David Murray, **34/5 (t)** Mr and Mrs Foulsham, Vale End/Derek St Romaine, **(b)** Garden Images, **35 (cb)** Wolf Garden, **37 (t)** Sainsbury's Homebase, **(bl)** David Murray, **39 (c)** Plantstuff, **40** Ray Main/Mainstream, **41 (l)** Jules Selmes, **(r)** Selective Marketplace, **42 (t)** John Lewis, **43** David Murray, **44** RHS Rosemoor, Devon/Derek St Romaine, **44/5** David Askham/GPL, **45 (c)** Wolf Garden, **(r)** JD Studios, **46 (l)** Hozelock, **47** Uniflex, **48 (t)** Gardena, **(b)** Tecnoma, **49 (l)** Selective Marketplace, **(r)** Bosmere, **50 (t)** Mary Evans Picture Library, **(c)** Plantstuff, **(l)** David Harber, **(b)** Selective Marketplace, **(br)** Jerry Harpur/David Harber, **52 (l)** Eden Greenhouses, **(r)** Agriframes, **53 (tl)** David Murray, **55 (c, r)** Jules Selmes, **56 (l)** Jules Selmes, **56/7** John Glover/GPL, **58 (tl)** Atco-Qualcast, **(tr)** Gardena, **59 (tl)** Jules Selmes, **59 (tr)** Gardena, **(br)** Husqvarna, **60 (tr)** Mary Evans Picture Library, **(cl)** Eric Crichton Photography, **(cr)** AKG London/Paul Almasy, **(bl)** David Murray, **(br)** Wolf Garden, **61** JulesSelmes, **62 (t)** David Murray, **(bl)** Gardena, **(br)** Husqvarna, **63 (t)** Hayter, **(bl, br)** Jules Selmes, **64 (t)** JD Studios, **(b)** Plantstuff, **65 (tr)** Jules Selmes, **(b)** David Murray, **66 (t)** Gardena, **(b)** Wolf Garden, **67 (b)** Howard Rice/GPL, **68/9** David Murray, **69 (b)** David Murray, **72** Gavin Kingcome/Gardens Illustrated Contributor Featherstone and Durber **74 (t)** Jules Selmes, **(b)** David Murray, **75 (l)** David Murray, **(r)** Jules Selmes, **76 (t)** JD Studios, **(b)** Castle Bytham,Lincolnshire/ Derek St Romaine, **77 (tl)** Greenfingers, **(tr)** Garden Images, **(b)** Andrea Jones/Garden Exposures, **78 (t)** Burgon and Ball, **(b)** Jacqui Hurst, **79 (l)** Jules Selmes, **81 (c)** Plantstuff, **82 (l)** David Murray, **82/3** Juliette Wade, **84 (bl)** David Murray, **86 (tr)** David Murray, **87** Plantstuff, **88/9** Jules Selmes, **90 (b)** M H Berlyn/Parasene **91** Garden Images, **93 (t)** Jules Selmes, **95 (c, r)** David Murray, **96 (l)** David Murray, **(r)** Juliette Wade, **97 (l)** David Murray, **(r)** Mel Yates, **99 (tr, b)** David Murray, **100 (r)** David Murray, **102** Andrew Lawson, **103 (t)** Gardena, **(c)** David Murray, **105 (r)** David Murray, **106 (tr)** AKG London, **(cl)** Howard Rice/GPL, **(cr)** Nicola Stocken Tomkins, **(bl)** Clive Nichols, **(br)** Fort Wheelbarrows, **107 (tl)** David Murray, **(b)** Agriframes, **108 (t)** Agriframes, **(b)** David Murray, **109 (tr)** David Murray, **110 (l)** David Murray, **111** Paul Felix, **112** David Murray, **113 (c, b)** David Murray, **114** David Murray, **115 (l)** Agralan, **(r)** Christopher Fairweather/GPL, **117 (l)** R K Alliston, **(c)** Garden Images, **(r)** Jules Selmes, **118** David Murray, **119 (tl)** Plantstuff, **(tr)** Clive Nichols, **120 (t, bl)** Plantstuff, **(br)** David Murray, **121 (tl)** R K Alliston, **(tr)** Plantstuff, **(bl)** David Murray, **(br)** Plantstuff, **122** Ray Main/Mainstream, **123** David Murray, **124** Town and Country, **125** Garden Images, **126** Jules Selmes, **127** Jules Selmes, **128 (l)** K Balls, **(r)** Jules Selmes, **129 (t)** Jules Selmes, **(b)** GettyOne Stone, **131 (l,r)** David Murray, **132** Draper Tools, **133 (bl, r)** David Murray, **134** David Murray, **135** David Murray, **136** Linda Burgess/GPL, **136/7** JD Studios, **137** JD Studios, **138** Howard Rice/GPL, **139** David Murray, **140** David Murray, **142 (t)** Hozelock, **(bl)** Burgon and Ball, **(br)** David Murray, **143 (l)** Plantstuff, **(r)** David Murray, **145 (l)** Plantstuff, **(c, r)** Jules Selmes, **146 (l)** Jules Selmes, **(r)** GPL, **147** Plantstuff, **148** Jules Selmes, **149 (l)** David Murray, **150 (l)** Garden Images, **(c,r)** Agriframes, **151** Jules Selmes

Jacket, front (tl, b) and back (r) David Murray

Suppliers

Carroll & Brown would particularly like to thank the following companies for supplying invaluable information and images. Many items are stocked by garden centres. Contact companies to find your nearest stockist.

Digging, cultivating, cutting and general tools

Bahco Tools
0121 504 5200
www.bahco.com

Burgon & Ball
01202 68 4141
www.burgonandball.com

Burton McCall
0116 234 4622
www.burton-mccall.co.uk

C.K Tools
01758 701070
www.ck-tools.com

Darlac Products
01753 547790
www.darlac.com

Draper Tools
023 8049 4333
www.draper.co.uk

Featherstone + Durber
0114 250 0180
www.featherstoneanddurber.co.uk

Gardena UK
0191 217 1537
www.gardena.com

Joseph Enterprises
01494 464653
www.josephenterprises.co.uk

Link-Stakes
01327 260329
www.link-stakes.co.uk

Nortene
01244 346193
www.nortene.com

Peta UK
01245 231811
www.peta-ukcom/index.html

Record Bulldog Tools
0114 244 9066
www.bulldogtools.co.uk

Sneeboer & ZN
00 31 (0)228 511 365
www.sneeboer.com

Spear & Jackson
0114 281 4242
www.spear-and-jackson.co.uk

Wilkinson Sword: Fiskars UK
01656 655595
www.fiskars.com

Wolf Garden
01495 306600
www.wolf-garden.co.uk

Chain saws
Husqvarna Forest & Garden
01453 822382
www.husqvarna.com

Andreas Stihl
01276 20202
www.stihl.co.uk

Watering equipment

Bonnington Plastics
01332 811811
www.bonningtonplastics.com

Gardena (see above)

Hozelock
01844 291881
www.hozelock.com

Plysu Brands
01234 841881
www.wardproducts.co.uk

Tecnoma
00 33 (0)4 74 62 48 48
www.tecnoma.fr

Uniflex
01424 427 691 (distributor)
www.uniflexutiltime.com

Weather watch

Diplex
01923 231784
Diplexexperience@amserve.net (email)

David Harber
01491 576956
www.davidharbersundials.co.uk

Greenhouse accessories

Agralan
01285 860015
agralan@cybermail.uk.com (email)

M.H. Berlyn
01384 896666
www.parasene.com

Eden Greenhouses
01242 676625
www.eden-greenhouses.co.uk

Harcostar Garden Products
01480 52323
www.harcostar.co.uk

H. E. Knowles
01384 78877

Netlon Sentinel
0114 5555
sales@netlon-sentinel.demon.co.uk
(email)

Synprodo Plantpak
01621 745 500
www.ukexnet.co.uk/hort/cha/synprod
o.htm

Two Wests & Elliott
01246 451077
www.twowests.co.uk

Lawn care

Atco-Qualcast
01449 742130
www.qualcast.co.uk

Greenacres
01895 835 235
sales@pzproducts.co.uk (email)

Hayter
01279 723444
www.hayter.co.uk

K-balls
01225 891 141
www.k-balls.com

Husqvarna Forest & Garden (see above)

Wolf Garden (see above)

Pond safety

Safapond
01636 815 777
roland@caleyco.demon.co.uk (email)

Clearing and tidying

Atco-Qualcast (see above)

Bosmere Products
01489 877566
www.bosmere.com

J. B. Corrie
01730 237100
www.jbcorrie.co.uk

FORT Wheelbarrows
01483 727898
www.fort-uk.com

H. E. Knowles (see greenhouse accessories)

Diamond Printed Products
01622 871666
Diamondim@aol.com (email)

Globe Organic Services
0121707 4120
www.globeorganic.co.uk

Haemmerlin
01384 243243.
www.haemmerlin.ltd.uk

Plant Trolleys
01424 819381
Web:www.plant-trolley.com

Blowers & vacuums

Flymo
01325 300303
www.flymo.com

Black & Decker
www.blackanddecker.com

Husqvarna (see above)

Andreas Stihl (see above)

Compost bins

Blackwall
0113 201 8000
www.blackwall.ltd.uk

Globe Organic Services (see above)

H. E. Knowles (see above)

Harcostar Garden Products
(see above)

Sankey
0115 927 7335
www.rsankey.co.uk

Ladders, platforms

Henchman
01635 299847
platforms@henchman.co.uk (email)

Footwear

Anderson & Firmin
01685 814000
aandf@globalnet.co.uk (email)

Hawkshead
0870 543 4000
www.hawkshead.com

Lakeland Footwear
020 8203 3983
www.lakepolo.co.uk

Millets
0800 214890
millets.co.uk

Tenax
01978 664667

Town & Country
01530 830990
www.townandco.com

Gloves

Anderson & Firmin (see above)

Centre Sales
0121 427 1992
www.centresalesgloves.co.uk

Stormafit
01284 811365

Town & Country (see above)

Wells Lamont
01765 640 940

Clothing

Aigle
020 7439 3565
www.aigle.com

J. Barbour
0191 455 4444
www.barbour.com

Haven Country Classics
01507 522113
sales@havencountryclassics.com
(email)

Hawkshead (see footwear)

Musto
01268 495830
www.musto.co.uk

Stormafit (see Gloves)

Sheds, tool storage racks

Store More Garden Buildings
0161 430 3347
storemore@care4free.net (email)

Backwoodsman
01631 720539
www.pyramidsarebetter.com

Larch-Lap
01299 251725.

Mail order and other specialists

Agriframes
01342 310000
www.agriframes.co.uk

Alberto Alessi
0207 518 9090
www.alessi.com

R K Alliston
www.rkalliston.com

Arabella Lennox-Boyd Garden Products Ltd
01524 771 838
www.arabellalennoxboyd.com

Earthworks
01306 502 007

English Gardenwares
01243 543804

Ferndown Lodge
01803 696500
www.ferndale-lodge.co.uk

Garden Images
01564 794035
www.garden-images.co.uk

The Garden Factory: Cannock Gates
01543 462500
www.cannock-gates.uk.com

Glenside Organics
01786 816655
enquiries@glensideorganics.demon
.co.uk (email)

Greenfingers
0845 302 3022
www.greenfingers.com

The Organic Gardening Catalogue
01932 253666
www.OrganicCatalog.com

Plantstuff
01458 851490
www.plantstuff.com

Queenswood Garden Products
01432 830015
www.queenswood.co.uk

Selective Marketplace
020 7620 2006

The Traditional Garden Supply Co.
0870 600 3366
sales@scottsofstow.demon.co.uk
(email)

Nurseries

Carpenders Park Nursery
020 8420 1959
www.carpenders-park-
nursery.co.uk

Dai-ichi Bonsai
01635 200667
www.dai-ichibonsai.com

David Austin Roses
01902 376300
www.davidaustinroses.com

Greenhouse
020 8905 9189

Shops

John Lewis (see local phone directory)

Sainsburys Homebase (see local phone directory)

Thistles Florists
01306 883800

If you need specialist tools and advice when gardening, contact:
Thrive
0118 988 5677
www.thrive.org.uk

Index

acid soil 93
activators, compost 114
aerating lawn 141–2
aerating soil 10, 32, 135, 138
aerators
    compost 115
    lawn 65–6, 142
algae clearance from ponds 103
alkaline soil 93
allergies 127
American shaker brush 97
American shovel 17
ankle boots 119–20
anvil pruner 138
anvil secateurs 14, 69–70
apex shed 151
aprons 121, 143
aquaplanters 103
arches 92
armillary sphere sundial 50
arms, protection 120–1
artificial fertilizers 112
artificial flowers 89
asparagus knife 35
atmospheric pressure measurement
    51
automatic vent openers for green-
    house 53
automatic watering systems 143
axes 79
    sharpening 149

bags
    fruit harvesting 45
    self-opening and collapsing 109
    transport 108–10
bamboo stakes 91, 92
barbecue safety 127
barometers 51
barrows see wheelbarrows
basket frames for rose training 15
baskets
    for harvesting 45, 104, 110
    for ponds 103
battery-powered cordless hedge
    trimmers 74
battery-powered mowers 59
    maintenance 148
bedding mattock 19
besom broom 96–7
bicycle-handled fork 134, 135
billhooks 79
bird protection of fruit 44–5
blade adjuster on mowers 61
blade and half-anvil secateurs 70
blades
    billhooks 79
    cleaning 147
    hedge trimmers 149
    knives 73
    mowers, maintenance 147, 148
    sharpening 62, 148–9
    saws 75
    scythes 78

secateurs 69, 71
    shears 74, 140
blinds for greenhouse 52–3
blowers 99–101
bonsai tools 28–9
boot rack 120
boots 119–21
    steel-toed, for chain saws 78
border fork 18, 21
border shears 64, 65
border spade 12
bouquets 89
bow saws 75
brambles, scything 79
branches
    pruning 75
    shredding 101
brass fittings for hoses 43
bristles on brooms 96, 97
brooms 96–8
    besom 96–7
    children's 123
    handles 96, 97–8
    patio 97
    push 96, 97–8
brush hooks 79
brushes 96–8
    American shaker 97
    bonsai 29
    for mower maintenance 147
bubble polythene 53
buckets 92, 143
    cut flowers 88
    fruit harvesting 45
    transport 108–10
Budding, Edwin Beard 60
budding knife 15, 45, 73
    for flower arranging 89
budgeting for tools 136–7
bulb planters 85
bulbs
    dibber for 86
    planting 84
butts 48
Buxus sempervirens 76
bypass pruners 138
bypass secateurs 68–70

cables, checking 147
calibrated trowel 84
canes 92, 143
canvas baskets 110
canvas tray in wheelbarrow 107
carbon-steel tools 23
    hand forks 85
    trowels 85
carts 107–8
celery, earthing up 35
cement bags, moving around 107
chain saws 78
    safety 129
    sharpening 149
chemicals, safety 127, 129
chest, protection 120–1

chicken wire
    compost bins 113
    flower arranging 88, 89
    topiary 77
children
    in gardens, safety 127
    tools 122–3
        digging 122
        plantings 123
        rakes 123
chisel for bonsai 29
choosing tools 20–1, 23
    hand tools 27, 33, 36
    secateurs 69–71
clamps for bonsai 29
cleaning tools 146–8
clearing water in ponds 103
cloche tunnel 35
cloches 91
clogs 119–20
clothing, protective 118–26
    chest, arms and legs 120–1
    children's 123
    feet 119–20
    hands 124–5
    head and face 126
    for using chain saws 129
cold frames 91
coloured tools for easy finding 143
comfrey leaves for composting 114
compacted turf, aerating 141–2
compost bags, moving around 107
compost bins 113–15
    insulation 114–15
    making 114
    siting 115
compost fork 115
compost tumbler 113–14
composting 112–15
    compost bins 113–15
    making a heap 115
    materials for 114
    success with 114–15
    turning materials 115
compressed air pruners 138–9
computerized watering system 143
concrete mixing, shovel 17
concrete shed 151
conifer pruning 74
connectors for hoses 43, 143
conservatories 52–3
container plants
    drip-feed system for 47, 143
    water needs 40, 41
containers 92–3
    bonsai 29
convector heaters 53
cordless shears 140, 141
cork toppers for canes 143
Cornish spade 17
costs of tools 23, 136
covers for ponds 103
cowhide gloves 125
craft knife for flowers 88

cultivating, specialized tools for
    134–5, 138
cultivators 32, 35
    mini- 138
    pistol-grip 135
    specialized 135–6
    three-prong 37
    wheeled hoe 27, 30
current device 128
cut-and-grip pruners 138
cutters for bonsai 29
cutting tools 68–71
    axes and hatchets 79
    billhooks 79
    chain saws 78
    for flowers 88
    hedge tools 73–5
    knives 71–3
    large 75, 78–9
    loppers 71
    saws 75, 78
    scythe 78–9
    secateurs 68–71
    shears 73–4
    shredders 79
    sickle 79
    small 71, 73
    specialized tools 138–40
    see also pruning and under specific
        tools
cuttings
    from shredders 101
    knives for 73
    propagators 90–1
cylinder mower 56, 58, 60, 61
    maintenance 148
    specialized 140

daisy grubber 65
deadheading roses 14
deerskin gloves 125
dew on lawn 57
D-handles 21
dibbers 35, 85–6
digging
    double 10, 16
    need for 10
    safety 129
    single 10, 13, 15
digging tools
    children's 122
    specialized 134–5, 138
digging up plants 13
digital thermometers 51
diluters for hoses 14, 44
disabilities, tools for 142–3
dispenser, seed 34, 35
distilled water for mower batteries
    148
dividing plants 85
dollies for transporting 107
dot matrix shading film 53
double-check valve 143
double digging 10, 16

double-lever secateurs and loppers 44
dowels for storage 150
drainage 10
draw hoe 27, 30, 35
dried flowers 89
drill marking 83
drilling safety 129
drip-feed systems 44–5, 143
    for greenhouse 52
    for hanging baskets 143
dual-purpose shed 151
Dutch hoe 27, 137

ear defenders 78, 101, 126
earplugs 126
edging tools 64–5
    half-moon 56, 65
    specialized 140–1
Egyptian sundial 50
electric blower/vacuum 100
electric chain saw 78
electric flame gun 134
electric heaters 53
electric hedge trimmers 74
    with telescopic arm 137
electric mowers 58
    hover mowers 140
    maintenance 147
electric propagators 91
electric scarifiers 141
electric shredders 101
electric sprayers 48
electricity, safety 128–9
English Garden spade 12
English pruning saws 76
expanding rakes 98, 99
eye protection see goggles

fabric gloves 124
    modern 125–6
fabric scissors 89
face protection 126
fan heaters 53
fan rake 66, 98–9
    small 98
fatigue, dealing with 134
feeder, hose-end 14, 44
feet, protection 119–20
ferrules 33
fertilizer bags for compost 113
fibreglass pots 93
Ficus pumila 76
files for sharpening 149
filters for ponds 103
finding tools easily 143
finials for hoses 44
fish removal from ponds 103
flail mower 58, 63
flame wands/guns 133, 134
fleece clothing 121
fleece for protecting roses 15
flexible rake 66–7
floral foam for flower arranging 89
floral scissors 71
    short-blade 88
flowers

arranging 88–9
artificial 89
carrying 110
dried 89
keeping fresh 88
foam for flower arranging 89
folding framed wheelbarrow 107
forcing pot 35
forks 12, 18–19, 136
    bicycle-handled 134, 135
    border 18, 21
    choosing 20–1, 23
    compost/manure 115
    garden 18
    hand 33, 36–7, 122, 137
    handles 21
    hay 18
    joints 20, 21
    lawn aeration 18, 141–2
    long-handled hand fork 135
    manure 18
    pistol-grip 135
    pitch 18, 19
    potato/beetroot 18
    sizes 21, 23
    specialized 135
frost protection
    in greenhouse 53
    for roses 15
fruit cages 44–5
fruit-growing tools 44–5
fruit picker 45
fruit-picker's basket 110
fruit picking 71
futuristic tools
    hose trolley 48
    lawn mowers 59
    plastic 23, 37

gaiters for working with chain saws 129
galvanized steel
    buckets 109
    pots 93
    watering cans 42
galvanized zinc wire netting for fruit cage 45
garden fork 18
garden line 35, 83–4
garden saws 75
garden snips 71
gas flame wand 134
gas heaters 53
gear-handled shears 140
glass cloches 91
glasses see goggles
gloves 118, 124–6
    anatomy 124
    for chain saws 78, 129
    fabric 124
    house-plant mitts 124
    leather 125
    modern fabric 125–6
    pond 124
    for shredders 101
    storing 124
    for topiary 77

thornproof 126
vinyl 124
waterproof 125
for working with roses 15, 71
gnomon 50
goatskin gloves 125
goggles 118, 126
    for chain saws 78
    for shredders 101
    for working with roses 15
golf-club hoe 133
Gore-Tex
    in boots 120
    jackets 121
grabbing rakes 99
grafting knives 73
grape harvesting snips 71
grass clippings
    collection 98
    composting 113
grass cutting
    scythe 79
    shears 64, 74
    sickle 79
grass hook 79
grass tillering 57, 61
Grecian saws 76
greenhouse
    temperatures 51
    tools 52–3
        automatic vent openers 53
        capillary matting 52
        heaters 53
        insulation 52 , 53
        reservoirs 52
        self-watering trays 52
        shading 52–3
grinding stones 149
grippers for storing tools 150
grips on handles 21
grubbers 65
guides for hoses 44

hairpins for topiary 77
half-moon edger 56, 65
hand-forged spades 22
hand fork 36–7, 85, 137
    children's 122
    long-handled 135
handles on tools 21
    broom 96, 97–8
    dibbers 85–6
    quick-change systems 98–9, 100
hand mowers 58, 60, 61
hand protection 124–5
    see also gloves
hand tools 137
    for lawncare 64–7
    for weeding 27, 33, 36–7
hand trowels 84
hanging basket waterer 143
hard hat 126, 129
harpoon-like weed extractors 133
harvest
    carrying 104, 110
    children's 122
    fruit 45

hatchets 79
hats 119, 126, 129
hay fever 127
hay fork 18
head protection 126
heads of tools 23
heaters for greenhouse 53
Hedera helix 76
hedge shears for topiary 76
hedges
    billhooks 79
    cutting safety 128
    tools for 73–5
hedge trimmers 68, 74–5
    battery-powered cordless 74
    electric 74
    petrol-driven 74–5
    safety 127, 128
    sharpening 149
    specialized 139–40
    with telescopic arm 137
helmets 126, 129
    for chain saws 78
herbicide sprayers 48
hiring tools 68
hoeing, timing 31
hoes 12, 27, 30
    draw (swan-neck) 27, 30, 35
    Dutch 27, 30, 137
    golf-club 133
    onion 35, 37
    oscillating 30, 31
    pistol-grip 135
    sharpening 149
    triangular-headed 27, 30
    for vegetables 35
    wheeled 27, 30
hollow-tine aerator 142
holster for knives 147
hooks for storage 150
hose-end feeder 14
hose reels 44
    coloured 143
hoses 43–4
    connectors 43, 143
    diluters 14, 44
    drip-feed systems 44–5
    extensions 43, 48
    guides and finials 44
    lances and pistols 43, 48, 143
    non-return valves 46
    porous zig-zagged 142
    sprinklers 41, 43, 47–8
    trolley 48
    types 43
hot-air blowers 53
house-plant mitts 124
house plants, water needs 41
hover mower 60, 62
    maintenance 148
    safety 128
    specialized 140
Howard, Sir Albert 112
humidity 41, 43, 51
humus 112
hyacinth bulbs 123
hygrometers 51

Ilex aquifolium 76
insect repellents 127
insulation
    for compost bins 114–15
    for greenhouse 52, 53
iris, dividing 85
irons, edging 64

jackets 121, 129
joints of weeding tools 26–7
joints on tools 20, 21
    hand tools 33

kenzan, for flower arranging 89
kitchen waste, for composting 113
knapsack sprayers 15
kneel pads 118, 121, 134
kneeler stool 134
kneeling in comfort 134
knives 71–3
    asparagus 35
    budding 15, 45, 73 , 89
    craft 88
    grafting and cuttings 73
    handmade pocket 72
    holster 147
    long-armed weeding 133
    making 72
    protecting 147
    pruning 44, 68, 73
    sharpening 148, 149
knuckle protectors on saws 75
Ko Yu 106

labelling 82, 83, 84
lacewing chamber 115
ladder truck trolley 108
ladders, safety 127–8
lances for watering 43, 48, 143
lantern cloches 91
Laurus nobilis 76
lawncare 56–67
    aeration 65–6, 141–2
    brushing 97
    edging tools 64–5, 83, 140–1
    equipment safety 127
    grubbers 65
    hand tools 64–7
    mowing 57
        see also lawn mowers
    raking 66–7 , 97
    rollers 67
    scarifiers 66
    shears 64
    specialized tools for 140–2
    spiking 18, 19
    sprinklers 41, 43, 47–8, 49
    thatch removal 66
    turfing irons 67
    watering 43
lawn moss, scarifying 141
lawn mowers 58–63, 137
    blade adjuster 61
    blade sharpening 62
    cutting edges 59
    cutting height 61–2
    cylinder 56, 58, 59, 60, 140

electric-driven 58
flail 58, 63
history 60
hover 60, 62, 140
maintenance 147–8
manual 58, 60, 61
nylon-cord 58, 63
petrol-driven 58
power 58–9
reciprocating knife 58, 62, 63
reel 63
ride-on 60, 62
robotic 59
rollers 61
rotary 58, 59, 61–2, 140
safety 57, 61, 128
solar-powered 59
specialized 140
steam 60
lawn trimmers, safety 128
leaf collection 105
    blowers and vacuums 99–101
    grabbers 99
    from lawn 66
    from ponds 103
    rakes 98, 99
        children's 123
leaf composting 112–13
leaf cutters for bonsai 29
leather boots 120
leather gloves 125
left-handed pruners 137
legs, protection 120–1
leylandii pruning 74
lifting safely 129, 142
line, garden 35
liners for ponds 103
logs 78, 79
long-arm pruners 44, 71
long-armed weeding knife 133
long-handled hand fork 135
long-handled pruners 68, 137, 138
loppers 15, 71, 71
    double lever 44
    long-arm 71
    ratchet 44, 132, 138
    sharpening 148, 149

maintaining tools 146–51
Manaresi secateurs 70
manual *see* hand
manure for composting 112
manure fork 18, 115
masks 129
mason wasps 115
mattocks 19–20
    bedding 19
meadow, wildflower 56
measuring rods 83, 84
mercury thermometers 51
mesh netting for fruit cage 45
metal pots 90, 91, 93
metal shed 151
metal watering cans 42
metal wheelbarrows 106, 107
microclimates 41
mild steel tools 23

mini-cloches 87
mini-cultivator 138
misters 42–3
mobile sprinkler 47–8
modules 87, 90
moss, scarifying 141
mowers *see* lawn mowers
mowing 57
mulch 26
    from compost 115
    from shredders 101
mulching 133
multi-functional wheelbarrow 141
multi-purpose tool 100
mustard and cress hedgehog 123

nails for storing tools 150
nets for ponds 103
netting
    fruit cage 45
    shade 53
Nitrile gloves 125
nozzles for watering cans 42
nylon-cord trimmer 58, 63, 141

obelisk
    for plants 92
    for roses 15
    sundial 50
oil level checking 147
oiled sand for cleaning tools 146
onion hoe 35, 37
organic cycle 14
organic matter 10, 26, 112–13, 114
oscillating hoe 30, 31
oscillating sprinkler 47
overboots 120
overshoes for aerating lawn 65–6

paraffin heaters 53
parrot-bill secateurs *see* bypass
    secateurs
path, portable 35, 108
patio broom 97
pea sticks 92
peat pots 90
pent-roofed shed 151
pergolas 92
permanent wilting point 40
pesticide sprayers 48
petrol-driven equipment
    blower/vacuum 100–1
    chain saw 78
    hedge trimmers 74–5
    mowers 58, 60, 147–8
pH of soil 93
picks 19–20
pigskin gloves 125
pinholders for flower arranging 89
pistol-grip tools 135
pistols for watering 43
pitch fork 18, 19
plant dollies 107
planting 13
    ponds 102–3
    vegetables 34
planting tools 82–6

bulb planters 85
dibbers 85–6
garden line 83, 84
hand fork 85
labels 83, 84
measuring rods 82–3, 84
sieves 86, 87
trowels 84
plants
    dividing 85
    grouping 41
    need for water 40–1
    poisonous 127
    supports 91–2
    transplanting 87
    watering in greenhouse 52
    young, pots for 90
plastic bags for compost 113
plastic barrow 137
plastic buckets 109
plastic cloches 91
plastic compost bins 113
plastic dibbers 86
plastic netting for fruit cage 45
plastic pots 90, 93
plastic stakes 92
plastic tools 23, 37
plastic trellis 92
plastic watering cans 42
plastic wheelbarrow 106
platforms for hedge cutting 128
pliers for bonsai 29
plug plants, planting out 86
plunger weeder 134
pocket knives, handmade 72
poisonous plants 127
Polartex clothing 121
pole pruners 71
pollen count 127
polypropylene thread 83
polythene, bubble 53
pond gloves 124
Pond Pads 103
ponds 102–3
    safety 127
portable path 35, 108
posies 89
potato fork 18
potatoes, earthing up 35
pots 92–3
    choosing 92–3
    for seedlings and young plants
        90
potting 82–93
    planting tools 82–6
    pots and containers 92–3
    propagating tools 87, 90–2
potting bench 82
power tool safety 128–9
pricking out 86
propagating tools 87, 90–2
    basic kit 87
    cloches and cold frames 91
    knives 73
    modules 87, 90
    pots for seedlings and young
        plants 90

propagators 90–1
seed trays 87, 87
supports 91–2
propagators 90–1
Pro-seeder 35
protective clothing 118–26
chest, arms and legs 120–1
feet 119–20
hands 124–5
head and face 126, 128
using chain saws 129
pruners
anvil 138
bypass 138
compressed air 138–7
cut-and-grip 138
left-handed 137
long-arm 44
long-handled 68, 138, 137
ratchet 44, 137, 138
side-anvil 14
pruning
bonsai 28
fruit 44
roses 14
see also cutting
pruning saws 75
sharpening 148
pruning tools 68–71
knife 44, 73
loppers 71
secateurs 68–71
specialized 138–40
see also pruners
prunings, shredding 79, 100, 101
pull-action saw 44
pumps for ponds 102, 103
push brooms 96, 97–8
push-pull weeders 133
PVC boots 120
PVC lawn rake 97

quick change systems for tools
97–8, 100

rain gauges 49, 51
rakes 31–2, , 98–9, 136–7
children's 123
expanding 98, 99
fan 66, 98
flexible 66–7
grabbing 99
for lawn 66–7
small fan 98
small sweep 98
springbok 66
teeth number 32
three-pronged, for bonsai 29
raking 31
ratchet lopper 44, 132, 138
ratchet pruners 44, 138, 137
ratchet secateurs 44, 70, 138
reap hook 79
reciprocating knife mower 58, 62,
63
reel mower 63
reels, hose 44, 143

refuse cart 110
reservoirs for greenhouse 52
residual current device 57, 128
rhubarb forcing pot 35
ribbon for flower arranging 89
riddle 86
ride-on mower 60, 62
right-angled trowel 84
robotic lawn mower 59
roller blinds 53
rollers
for lawn 67
on mowers 61
roll-out paths 35, 108
rootball spade 12
roses 14–15
pruning ground-cover type 70
roses for watering cans 42
rotary mower 58, 59, 61–2
maintenance 148
specialized 140
rotary sprinkler 47, 48
rotary-hammer 47
rubber buckets 109
rubber toppers for canes 143
rust
curing 148
inhibition 147

sack truck 108
saddle joint 21
safety 127–9
chain saws 78, 129
chemicals 127, 129
children in gardens 127
clothing 118–26, 128
electricity 128–9
hedge trimmers 127, 128
knives 147
ladders 127–8
lawn mowers 57, 128
lawn trimmers 128
lifting 129, 142
residual current device 128
saws 75
secateurs 69
shed 151
shredders 101, 129
working with roses 15
sand for cleaning tools 146
sandpits 127
saws 75–9, 138
bow 75
chain 76
English pruning 76
garden 75
Grecian 76
pruning 15, 75
pull-action 44
sharpening 148
straight-bladed 76
scarifiers 66, 141
scissors
bonsai 29
fabric 89
floral 71
short-bladed floral 88

topiary 76–7
vine 44, 45
scoop, soil 83
scorch 41
scorching weeds 134
scraper for mower maintenance
147
screw clamp for bonsai 29
screws for storing tools 150
scuffle hoe see Dutch hoe
scythes 78–9
sharpening 149
secateurs 68–71, 137
anvil 14, 69, 70
blade and half-anvil 70
bypass 68, 70
choosing 69–70
double-lever 44
flowers 88, 89
how to use 70–1
Manaresi 70
pruning roses 14
ratchet 44, 70, 138
sharpening 148, 149
topiary 76–7
second-hand tools 136
seedbed preparation 31, 85
seedlings
dibbers for 86
pots for 90
watering 42
Seedmaster 35
seeds
dispenser 34
labelling 83
propagators 90, 91
sowing 83, 86
seed tray 87
predivided 87
self-opening and collapsing bag 109
self-watering trays 52
shading for greenhouse 52–3
shaker brush 97
sharpening tools 148–9
shears 64
anatomy 64
border 64, 65
cordless 140, 141
edging 64
gear-handled 140
grass 64, 65, 74
hedging 73–5, 138–7
hand-operated 73–4
single-handed 74
topiary 76, 77
pruning 15, 68
sharpening 149
single-handed 141
single-shafted 141
sheds 150–1
locking 127
safety 151
size 150–1
types 151
sheets for transport 108–10
tip-type 110
shock absorbers

secateurs 70
shears 74
shoes 119–20
short-bladed floral scissors 88
shovels 10, 12, 17
American 17
children's 122
Cornish 17
mixing concrete 17
shredders 79, 100, 101
safety 129
shrub pruning 70
sickles 79
sharpening 149
side-anvil pruners 14
sieves 86, 87
sight, poor, specialized tools for
132, 143
single digging 10, 13, 16
single-handed shears 74, 141
single-shafted shears 141
sizes of tools 21, 23
skimmers 103
slashers 79
Smith, Thomas 111
snips, garden 71
socket joint 21
soil
compaction relief 19, 32
crumbler 135–6
drainage 10
improvement 10–25, 135
levelling 19
organisms 10, 26
preparation for planting 82
scoop 83
testing 93
solar-powered lawn mower 59
sowing seed 83, 86
spade 10, 12–16, 136
anatomy 12
border 12
children's 122
choosing 20–1, 23
English Garden 12
handles 21
joints 20, 21
manufacturing 22–3
pistol-grip 135
rootball 12
sharpening 149
sizes 21, 23
specialized 135
specialized tools 133–45
carrying water 142–3
digging and cultivating 134–5,
138
kneeling comfort 134
lawns 140–2
for poor sight 143
pruning and cutting 138–40
weed control 133–4
spiking lawn 65–6
spine protection 129, 142
sprayers 48
hose-end feeder 14
knapsack 15

spray wand *see* lance
spraying trees 48
springbok rake 66
sprinklers 41, 43, 47–8, 49
   mobile 47–8
   oscillating 47
   rotary 47, 48
   rotary-hammer 47
   static (spike) 47
stainless-steel tools 23
staking 91–2
static (spike) sprinkler 47
steam mowers 60
steel grippers for storing tools 150
steel toe caps on boots 120, 129
stepladder truck trolley 108
Stevenson screen 49
stone pots 93
stool, kneeler 134
storing tools 149–50
straight-bladed saws 76
straw for composting 112–13
sundials 50
sunscreens 127
supports for plants 91–2
Sussex trugs 111
swan-neck hoe *see* draw hoe
sweep rakes, small 98

tang 33
taps for hoses 43, 143
Taxus baccata 76
telescopic arm 45
   electric hedge trimmers with 137
terracotta pots 93
T-handle 21
thermometers 49, 51
   compost 115
Thinsulate gloves 125
thornproof gloves 126
three-pronged cultivator 37
three-pronged rake for bonsai 29
tidying gardens 96–101
   blowers and vacuums 99–101
   brooms 96–8
   rakes 98–9
   shredders 100, 101
ties, tree 45
tillering 57, 61
tilth, preparation 82, 86, 87
time, sundials 50
tip sheet 110
toe caps on boots 120, 129
tool bags 150
tool belt holder 143
tool box on wheelbarrow 107
topiary
   shears 77, 141
   tool kit 76–7
toppers for canes 143
training weeping roses 15
transplanting 87
   trowel 84
transport tools 104–11
   buckets, bags, and sheets
      108–10
   carts and trolleys 107–8

sack truck 108
   trugs and baskets 104, 110–11
   wheelbarrows 104–7
trays, self-watering 52
tree clamp for bonsai 28, 29
trees
   pruning 75, 78
   spraying 48
   staking 92
   stumps 79
   ties 45
   topiary 76–7
trellis 92
trenches
   digging 16
   earthing up 35
triangular-headed hoe 27, 30
trimmer 58, 63, 63
   hedge 68, 74–5, 149
   safety 128
   specialized 139–40, 141
   with telescopic arm 137
trolleys 107–8
   for hoses 48
trousers
   for working with chain saws 78,
      129
trowels 33, 36, 84, 137
   anatomy 36
   bulb-planting 85
   calibrated 84
   children's 122
   hand 84
   pistol-grip 135
   right-angled 84
   transplanting 84
truck trolley, stepladder 108
trugs 110
   making 111
tub trug 110
tubs, moving around 107
tumbler, compost 113–14
tunnel cloche 35, 91
turf skimming 16
turfing irons 67
turntable for flower arranging 89
tweezers for bonsai 28, 29
twigs, shredding 101
twine 15, 83
tyres on wheelbarrows 105, 106,
   107

umbrella baskets for rose training
   15
underlays in ponds 103
urns 92
UV clarifiers 103

vacuums 99–101
   for ponds 103
valves
   double check 143
   non-return 44
vegetable grower's tools 34–5
vegetable seed sowing 83
ventilation in greenhouse 52
   automatic 52, 53

vents in propagators 91
Victorian cloches 91
vine scissors 44, 45
vines, pruning 70
vinyl gloves 124

waders 103, 118, 120, 121
washing dirty tools 146–7
water
   carrying 142–3
   distilled, for mower batteries 148
   filters for watering 143
   plants' need for 40–1
   pressure reducers 143
   test sets 103
water features 102–3
   clear water 103
   design 102
   liners 103
   planting 102–3
   pumps 102
watering
   automated systems 41
   greenhouse 52
   timing 41
   tools for 40–9
      butts 48
      containers 47
      drip-feed systems 44–5, 143
      hoses 43–4
      humidity and water loss 41
      misters 42–3
      plant needs 40–1
      sprayers 48
      sprinklers 41, 43, 47–8
      when to water 41
watering cans 41, 42, 137
   children's 123,
   for flower arrangements 89
   rectangular plastic 142, 143
   specialized 142
waterlogging 10
waterproof gloves 125
weather stations 49, 49, 51
weeding tools 26–37
   fork 135
   grubbers 65
   knife, long-armed 133
   pistol-grip weeder 135
   plunger weeder 134
   push-pull weeder 133
   specialized tools for 133–4
   weed extractor 133
   weed puller 134
weeds
   scorching 134
   skimming 16
weeping roses 15
Weil's disease risk 124
Wellington boots 118, 119
   children's 123
wheelbarrows 104–7, 137
   anatomy 105
   children's 123
   folding framed 107
   history 106
   metal 107

   multi-functional 141
   wooden 105, 106
wheelchair gardening 132
wheeled hoe 27, 30
whitewashing greenhouse 53
widgers 86
wigwams 92
wildflower meadow 56
wilting 40–1
wind speed and direction
      measurement 51
wire
   for bonsai 29
   for flower arranging 88, 89
wire baskets 110
wire cutters
   for bonsai 29
   for flower arranging 88
wire frame for topiary 77
wire mesh compost bins 113
wooden baskets 110
wooden compost bins 113
wooden containers 93
wooden handles, preservation of
   147
wooden shed 151
wooden stakes 92
wooden wheelbarrow 105

YD-handle 21